I Found Me: The Woman I've Become

# I Found Me: The Woman I've Become

Angie Ford

For my sister, Tonya—my first cheerleader.
You believed in me long before I believed in myself.
Your love carried me through storms you never even knew I was fighting.
Rest in the bosom of the Lord, beautiful.
Your faith in me lives in these pages.

And for Mrs. Jackson.
You saw the child I was and the woman I became.
You named my resilience when I didn't have the language for it.
Your words opened a window in my mind and let the truth in.
Thank you for seeing me. Rest in paradise.

# Contents

# Introduction

Why am I writing this memoir now?

Because healing finally demanded honesty.

Putting these memories on paper has been my way of processing trauma, releasing secrets, and making sense of a life I spent years surviving instead of understanding. Writing became a form of emotional healing and catharsis. It has allowed me to process traumatic events, manage stress, and embrace emotional closure. I have gained a different perspective of my life. I understand my past, I have made sense of my life's journey, and I would certainly call this phase self-discovery and understanding.

I wrote this memoir for anyone who has ever felt lost, silenced, overlooked, or broken. If my story helps even one person feel less alone in their grief, their confusion, or their becoming, then every page was worth it. I also wrote it to tell my own version of events; the version I silently carried for years. Some of these stories were secrets. Some were wounds. All of them shaped me.

To anyone I've had a relationship with on any level whether it was family, friends, or those I believed were in monogamous relationships with me, I have no harsh words for you. I simply want to say thank you. Thank you for the lessons. Thank you for making me realize my worth. Thank you for showing me that I deserved better. Thank you for leaving, so I could find the parts of myself I had lost. I carry the memories, but they no longer make me sad.

This book taught me to guard the word *friend* more carefully. Writing has revealed that some people I once wanted to sit beside may have never liked me… it's also taught me that I never needed their table.

Not for validation. Not for belonging. Not for anything. I finally understand why my lack of need bothered people. When I stopped waiting for permission and stopped begging for a seat, I stopped shrinking to make others comfortable. It was never my responsibility to manage their discomfort with my truth.

This last year made that clear. God wasn't trying to fit me into rooms. He was building something through obedience, process, pain, and consistency… long before there was any applause. I've learned to bless people who never blessed me, to clap for people who would never consider clapping for me, and to keep my mouth shut while God handles the results. Not because I'm better, but because I'm called.

Hence, *the woman I've become.*

This is mission over applause. Obedience over validation; so, I finally said to myself, "Angie, if God told you to build, stop asking who's hosting the dinner. Pick up the tools and build what He showed you. The table comes later."

# Ages 15 to 18

It was December 1987, and high school was out for winter break. The quiet of the evening at home made me restless enough to walk over to my neighbor Gloria's house, just across the street. When I stepped outside, I felt the North Carolina cold hit my face—it was 30 degrees—followed by the smell of burning wood coming from the neighbors' chimney. Some people loved the smell of wood burning, but not me. It felt like the smoke pierced straight through my lungs.

We lived on the Westside of Charlotte, on a street called Justice Avenue that nestled in the neighborhood of Druid Hills. The neighbors with the fireplace lived in the house to the right of our duplex. To the left of us stood a Holiness church that I visited regularly, to escape mental and verbal abuse.

Ironic to live on a street called Justice, when I received little to no justice.

The streetlight was dim and struggling to light the way. The road was empty, and dogs were barking somewhere in the distance.

I walked faster to escape the cold. The night was frigid enough to make my breath visible, and I chuckled at myself for thinking that it looked like I was smoking.

I was finally up the steps and on Gloria's porch, knocking at her front door. The smell of her kerosene heater was so heavy that it greeted me before she opened the door.

I stepped inside and greeted her four-year-old son and her cousin, believing I was in a familiar place. My parents trusted Gloria because they thought they knew her, and I carried that trust with me.

Gloria was short, with caramel brown skin and naturally curly hair.

She was heavy up top and got slender toward her bottom. Honestly, not to sound mean, but she was built like Gru from *Despicable Me* except with breasts. Her house was at least 30 years old and in desperate need of a makeover. Sheets were hung at the windows instead of curtains. The furniture looked like it had come from the Salvation Army.

Gloria and her cousin were hanging out, drinking and listening to the radio. Her son was watching something on their floor-model TV. The kerosene odor kept pressing against my temples until my head began to throb. When I mentioned I had a headache from the kerosene fumes, someone offered me a drink of Thunderbird, as if it would help ease the pain.

I remember exactly what I wore that night, because my father had told me that I looked like a tomboy because I was wearing sweats and sneakers. I am five feet, seven and three quarter inches, so I always say that I am 5'8". Back then, I wore my hair in a wave nouveau, it was similar to a Jheri Curl, but the process gave my hair more of a wavy pattern. I was a plus-sized teenager, and weighed 220 pounds. I always felt self-conscious because my father was always a negative person and never said anything to encourage me. On this particular night, I was wearing a Coca-Cola sweatshirt, which I'd purchased during a trip to Atlanta earlier that year, along with white sweatpants, red and white socks, and white Reeboks. I felt proud of how I looked, because I wasn't half dressed, showing cleavage, thighs, or my behind.

But lasciviousness doesn't care how you are dressed, and I was unaware of how quickly the night would turn.

I was only 15. I had no business hanging with such an older crowd.

At some point, I accepted the Thunderbird—a wine that has a higher alcohol content than other wines, but of course I didn't know that. And if I'm being honest, I don't know how many drinks I was given and ended up drinking. I didn't know what I was supposed to feel as I drank that horrible wine, but I do remember suddenly feeling like I was in a sauna.

It was so hot, and I got very drunk. I threw up all over my sweatshirt. At some point, I passed out.

For whatever reason, Gloria decided to leave her house, she put her son to bed, and that left me alone with her family member. His name was Harold Lee, a man who was old enough to be my father.

When I awakened from being passed out, his exact words were, "Wait a minute! I was about to get my nut!" It was like he'd been summoned from the pits of hell to take advantage of a teenage girl.

I had been compromised by this man. He was dark as midnight, short, with eyes that looked jaundiced, brownish-yellow teeth, and an indescribable stench.

I was in tears. I was furious! I got up as quickly as I could to leave the house.

As I was leaving, Gloria's "old man" was about to enter the house. His name was Robert. Robert was a little bit taller than Gloria, very dark-skinned and slender—the blackest, meanest old man I had ever laid eyes on. I told him that Harold Lee had just raped me. Robert looked me in my eyes and said, "Good! That's what you get, because you're a whore!"

I was baffled. Before that incident, I had never been sexually active. I was a virgin. That was the night that I lost my virginity.

Robert yelled more obscenities at me as I walked down the stairs from their front porch. And while I couldn't feel my legs, thank God, I managed to get myself off of their property before anything further could occur.

Everything around me seemed dark. I heard only my footsteps and my heart rapidly beating.

When I got back to our duplex, I stepped immediately into the living room, and closed the door behind me. I stood there and cried silently. My parents were asleep in their bedroom, which was the first room to the left, off of the living room. My room was next to theirs, and beside my room was the kitchen. On the other side of the kitchen wall was the only bathroom my parents and I shared. I stood in the living room, trembling. I was petrified; I was shaking so hard that the vibration made the ornaments on the Christmas tree sway. I stood for a moment overwhelmed with emotions.

I was scared to death to breathe a word of this to my parents. So, I hurried to my room and got undressed. I went to the bathroom and got in the shower and allowed the hot water run on me until it turned cold.

I was afraid to go to sleep. Every noise I heard, I was convinced that it was Harold Lee.

I was terrified of calling the police. I was too frightened to tell anyone.

The next day, when Gloria asked me what had happened, I told her even though I was still afraid. I don't know whether or not she believed me. She looked disappointed. I couldn't make sense of it. Was she disappointed in me? Or was she disappointed in herself for having left me alone in the house with Harold Lee?

I never returned to Gloria's home again. I realized that Gloria had never been my friend. She'd just been manipulating me.

Picking friends didn't come naturally to me. I wanted to feel accepted and understood, even though I didn't fully understand myself. I knew I wanted a real friend, someone I could share my secrets with and trust to keep them. Someone I could laugh and share jokes with.

Obviously, Gloria was not that person. Being much older than I was, she knew that I was naïve, so it was easy for her to manipulate me. Earlier that year, I had been involved in an auto accident, and had gotten maybe two thousand dollars in the settlement; Gloria knew this. She would tell some of the saddest stories, to make me feel so sorry for her and four-year-old son. She'd lie and say that they didn't have food, then ask me for money. I didn't know anything about food stamps back then, or that she was getting them. The money she was asking me for wasn't for food; it was to support her crack cocaine habit.

I was so green! And of course, I never got a dime of my money back.

At 15, I didn't know how to identify depression, but I sure knew what it felt like. I didn't know how to give voice to what I had experienced at Gloria's house, or what had happened at a much younger age, when I had been molested. That may very well be when I experienced depression for the first time. Sadly, when I told on the person who'd molested me, nothing was done to them.

No one believed me.

I felt like I had been silenced, and I knew in that moment that I would spend a lot of time trying to prove anything that was attached to my name. I mean, after all, a few months prior to me revealing this truth, I was accused of stealing from my mother.

It literally made me sick to my stomach and said that I hoped for once she'd believe me. My mother had wrongly accused me of stealing change from the console in her car.

I didn't even know she had money in her car!

I was so devastated by the false implication on my character, so I went outside, and sat on the ground, under the tree. This happened when we lived at 311 North Davidson Street, in the projects called Earle Village.

I cried. In between sobs, I said, "I wish I was a dog!" I hadn't wished to be a dog because of the physical nature of it, but because I understood even at that tender age that dogs received unconditional love, protection, and loyalty—and I was not getting those from the humans around me. I was not being childish. I was being a child trying to make sense of a world where trust was not safe.

Decades later, while earning my bachelor's degree in psychology I learned that some children experience what is called secondary enuresis. This happens when a child starts wetting the bed after being dry for at least six months.

Particular triggers for secondary enuresis are severe stress, emotional trauma, exposure to violence, or abuse—including sexual abuse. And I had all of those triggers.

I experienced severe stress—both of my parents cursed me out, but my father threatened me with an ass whipping almost daily.

Emotional trauma? In hindsight, I realize it was constant. I didn't grow up hearing "I love you," "You did a great job," or "I'm proud of you." My father was always yelling at me.

Abuse? My mother beat me for being a bedwetter. And I was sexually abused for the first time at six years old.

No one saw my bedwetting as a red flag, as a sign of trauma or abuse.

All my mother knew to do was to beat me.

I'm the youngest of four, so my brothers and my sister picked on me.

I felt isolated.

I felt unloved.

I felt like I had to constantly prove that I wasn't lying.

I was not a whore, regardless of what Robert said, and I was not wrong or imagining things.

Now that I look back over my life, I see that all the signs of depression were there from a young age. And my parents didn't recognize my depression, mostly because they were too busy playing the street lotto (which was illegal). They played and wrote numbers (they were bookies), like, three digit or four digit numbers, and if the number they played came out, they won what was equivalent to the amount they bet on the number.

Most days, I remained in my room, except for when I was at school or at church services next door.

When I returned to high school after the winter break was over, after what had happened at Gloria's house, I was still withdrawn. I didn't tell anyone at school what had happened to me. I was ashamed of myself, because Robert's words kept replaying in my mind: "You're a whore!" I didn't know if having been taken advantage of made me one or not; I just thought I was a whore because he'd said I was. I mean, he was older, so he would know, right?

My grades were deplorable. My grade-point average was less than one! If anyone would have told 15-year-old me that I would someday graduate from Liberty University with a bachelor's of science degree in psychology, I would have laughed at them.

The only three classes that intrigued me were Mrs. McCullough's algebra class, Mrs. Leake's psychology class, and Mr. Boyce's chorus class.

When a parent tells a child, "You ain't shit and will never be shit," it adds to the mental, verbal, and physical abuse they've already endured. It hurt my feelings to hear my own biological father utter those words to me. He made me feel unloved.

While I grew up with my father in my life, it felt like he was an absent father. And I say this because while he was physically present, he was emotionally and relationally absent. This is by no means an attempt to bash my father, instead it is to say that despite being in the home, he didn't provide guidance, attention, support, or meaningful involvement. As a matter of fact, Pastor Michael Todd speaks about the absent-present father in his sermon titled *I'm Tired of These Soul Ties* (this sermon is good and can be found on YouTube).

At the end of my sophomore year of high school, I falsified my birth certificate so that I could get a worker's permit, because back then, the law required me to be 16 years old before I could get a job. I knew I needed to get a job. My mother was on disability, so her income was very limited, and my father worked odd jobs, which meant his was scarce. Getting a job allowed me to purchase school supplies and the clothing that I needed for school.

Thank God I had sense enough to do that! After school and on the weekends, I began working as cashier at a fast-food restaurant. Then, during the summer, when that company found out my true age, I was terminated for having lied on my application. I didn't know to be embarrassed by the dismissal, but since my 16th birthday was within the next week or so, it didn't matter.

I ended up getting a job at Ryan's, a buffet-style restaurant about 10 miles away from our duplex. I worked there for nearly two years, taking two buses there and back each shift.

Here is a prime example of my father basically being absent, and of why he made me feel unloved. One night, I needed a ride from work. As my father, I thought he would have wanted to ensure my safety. I thought he was supposed to be my protector, and the person I could call on for help.

I couldn't have been more wrong.

When he answered the phone, I greeted him and told him that I needed a ride from work. It was after 10 p.m.

"How did you get there?" he asked me.

"I took the bus," I said.

"Well, hell, that's how you'll get your ass home!" he replied.

"I don't have any more money to take the bus," I said. I had used the only money in my pocket paying for the second bus to work that day, because waiting for the free-transfer bus would have made me late.

"That's your problem," father said. Then he hung up the phone.

Whenever one of his *friends* called him for a ride, he would go to them without hesitation! But not his own daughter.

There are several reasons I could not allow myself to be close to my father, and each reason leads back to something he'd done to wrong me.

For as long as I can remember, I never had a good relationship with him, because he did not try to establish a bond. He was not there for me as a man should have been for a child he had helped bring into this world.

He told me a funny thing once. Not funny "ha-ha," but funny because he didn't understand the magnitude of it. Just out of nowhere, one day he said to me, "I brought you into this world, and I will take you out."

The unnecessariness.

I was afraid to sneeze without permission, so the fact that he'd say something like that to me was insane. Those were the exact words that a news reporter claimed Marvin Gaye Sr. told his son, the singer Marvin Gaye Jr., before shooting and killing him.

I was not a bad child. Often misguided, but not bad.

I strongly disliked my father because of who he was and how he treated me. I loved him because he was my father, but I did not like him.

That night he refused to pick me up from Ryan's on Tyvola Road, so I learned what "pat and turner" meant. You pat one foot and turn the other. During the course of my nearly 10-mile-walk home, I remember stopping at the payphone to call 911 and let them know that I was walking the streets because my father wouldn't pick me up from work. The 911 operator told me, "The police is not a taxi service, ma'am!" She abruptly hung up the phone before I could utter another sound.

By this time, I was crying and talking out loud to myself, but by God's grace, I kept walking.

I had been walking for about eight miles when a pastor whom I had never met before, stopped and picked me up. He drove me the rest of the way home, about two miles. I remember him scolding me, saying that he had daughters my age and that I shouldn't have been out wandering the streets at that hour.

That pastor may very well have saved my life. Unsavory things happened in that area at night.

Not too long after that incident, we were padlocked out of our duplex for nonpayment of rent. My parents and I ended up going to stay a while at my mother's father's duplex, until my father paid the back rent in full.

I was working to pay for things any person would need each month—even food—because who was looking out for me? I also made sure I had school supplies and school clothes. I never thought to contribute to the household, because I was struggling just to make sure, I had what I needed.

Then, when we were finally back at our duplex, it was lights out and dry city!

Duke Energy had turned off the electricity, because the bill hadn't been paid. Our water had been shut off, too. Either one of my parents ordered me to go next door to the church to get water from the outside spigot.

By the time I was in my senior year of high school, my parents and I had moved to a different neighborhood. Once we had packed up everything, my father asked if we were forgetting anything, and I told him, "Our photo albums and vinyl records are still in that shed."

He said he'd return to get them. He lied.

We had crates of vinyl records and albums. The photo albums that had so many of my childhood memories inside were left behind. Everything about my birth was in one of the photo albums.

It was like none of it meant anything to him.

Our new neighborhood was within walking distance of Garinger High School, and I was already enrolled at Independence. So, my father told the principal at Independence Senior High School that the bus needed to pick me up in front of the Big Dipper restaurant on Shamrock Drive, so that I could get to school.

So, every morning, he would drive me a short distance to get on the school bus. But a ride beyond that half mile was completely out of the question.

Here's another prime example of his absenteeism.

My father knew that I wanted to go to my senior prom. Jennifer Metoyer, one of my schoolmates put me in touch with her grandmother, who was a seamstress. I bought the fabric and a dress pattern, went for my fittings, and *boom*!

The gown was beautiful!

It was an iridescent fabric; it looked black from one angle and royal blue from a different angle. It wasn't a snug fit, but it enhanced my curviness. I had on black pantyhose, black heels, and a blue wrist corsage.

Our former neighbor, Janice, a professional hairstylist, did my hair, makeup, and nails.

I looked so beautiful.

When I let my father know that I was ready to go, he said to me, "I am in my bed. I ain't stud'n bout taking you to no damn dance (*"stud'n"* meant he was the least bit concerned, and he was not about to drop me off at my prom). You better dance yo ass on in yo damn room." Janice even pleaded with him to take me to my prom, and all he said to her was, "She heard what the hell I told her to do. And that's all I'm gone say about that!"

I paid her for doing my hair, nails, and makeup.

I didn't want her to see me cry, so I excused myself and went to my bedroom.

My prom gown did eventually get used, though; someone called and asked me if they could use it for their wedding, and I told them that they could have it.

In May 1990, I was working at the Bi-Lo grocery store only a mile from the house, so I didn't mind walking. One day that month when I was at work, my mother suffered second- and third-degree burns. To my knowledge, my father had put her in the bathtub. She did not know how to operate the knobs, because it was still a new home to us.

While in the bath, she tried to turn the hot water on to get the water warmer. She panicked and kept turning the water toward hot.

My father was outside doing whatever it was he was doing and heard screaming, but he said later he thought it was the neighbor's children.

Mrs. Jackson, my mother's home health aide, called my job to inform me that my mother was in the ICU's burn unit.

Why didn't my father call me?

Why couldn't he be the one to tell me?

The day of my high school graduation, in June, my mother was still in the hospital, so she couldn't be there. Her father was there, and her auntie Sarah was there, but no one else from her family was there.

Neither of my siblings was there.

Once again, I felt alone.

My father was there, and two of his sisters, auntie Frances and auntie Ella Mae were there.

Being that I was in the school's choir, we had to sing on the day of our graduation, and my name was in the last group to be called. Independence had the largest graduating class in the county; there were 610 other people graduating. For a moment, Auntie Ella Mae thought I was not graduating, because she hadn't heard my name.

The school's choir was last because the organizers wanted to thank us for our last performance, and they wanted us to be recognized.

When my mother was released from the hospital, she was sent home with a hospital bed and a lot of bandages to provide wound care, but no instructions. Well, at least no one gave me any.

And my father told me again, just as he had told me when I was 15 years old, "Your mama is your responsibility." He meant that with every fiber of his being. He wanted to be responsible only for himself. Because here I was at 17 doing the work of a spouse who had taken vows that included "in sickness and in health."

You know what I learned from watching my father? I learned that I did not want to be married to a man like him.

Well, who do you suppose was my mother's caregiver again? I had initially become her caregiver when I was 12 years old, after she'd had an aneurysm.

Then, in 1990 when my mother was released from the hospital after being burned, my brother and his girlfriend (at the time) were at our house, doing absolutely nothing. In no way did either of them offer to lift a finger to help.

Time passed quickly, and here I was facing my 18th birthday. I stopped by my father's auto detailing shop. He had named it Angie's Auto Detailing. I guess I was supposed to be flattered by his gesture, naming it after me. But I was genuinely confused. He'd treated me like crap my whole life, and then decided to name a detailing shop after me? Like, make that make sense!

Anyway, I stopped by the auto detailing shop one day to pick up money to deposit at the bank. Billy, a hired hand who detailed the cars, was there.

At this point, my parents still did not know that Harold Lee had raped me three years prior. But now they found out, because Billy's nasty, disrespectful ass said to me, "Let me get some of that pussy!"

I was 18, and that dude was my father's *friend*! All of my flabbers had been gasted.

I was disgusted by the remark he'd made and told him no.

He asked me, "Why not? You gave Harold Lee some."

Before I got in my Mustang, I turned and looked him in his brown eyes and said to him, "Harold Lee raped me!"

And that was the first time I had ever said those words out loud for another person to hear them.

Billy told my father, who then asked me, "What were you wearing?"

When I heard him utter those words, I immediately felt like I was standing in direct sunlight. My stomach felt queasy, and I felt like I had thrown up in my mouth.

I told him, "It shouldn't have mattered if I walked around wearing nothing but a bright yellow wig. It was uncalled-for, for me to be raped by one of your so-called friends! I was a drunken teenager! A child!"

I couldn't believe he had allowed that backward thinking to come out of his mouth! But then he too would sit and stare at me like a damned pervert.

About two months later, the detailing shop flopped.

# My Six-Foot Teddy Bear

When I was 18, I went to work for a local distribution center for a while before becoming a school bus driver. Because I was so young at the time, I was often mistaken for a student. One day while waiting for the last bell to ring, I was on my way to the teacher's lounge when I saw the principal. He looked at me and said, "Hey, young lady. Oughtn't you be in class?"

I pulled out my Class B commercial driver's license to show him and said, "I drive that bus over there," as I pointed in the direction of my parked bus. His face turned beet red, he covered his mouth with both hands, and we had one really good belly laugh.

I had been driving the bus for maybe a month and a half when my mother's youngest brother, Karl, passed away in March 1992. Just a few months earlier, in October 1991, my mother's grandfather (we called him Paw-Paw) had passed away. I honored his legacy and sang "It's So Hard to Say Goodbye to Yesterday" by Boyz II Men.

Somewhere around that spring of 1992, I was called into the coordinator's office. This man looked like Boss Hog from the original *Dukes of Hazzard*! He proceeded to ask me if I had something to tell him. Well, being that he'd called me into his office, I wanted to say, "Don't you have something to tell me?" But I remained quiet.

He said, "I'll begin." He reared back in his office chair with his belly sitting in his lap and said, "I received a phone call from some fella doing some landscaping work who said you hit the wooden post in their center garden. Any truth to what he said?"

My heart started beating faster. I suddenly felt like I had diarrhea! I wanted to be anyplace but in that office. I said, "Yes. That did happen."

I could've easily blamed the distraction on the fact that my uncle had just passed, but I wanted to be honest. He told me that he was glad I admitted it, and that I would be on a probationary period, and the charges would be deducted from my paycheck.

The more seasoned drivers told me that he couldn't do that, but I was naïve and didn't know if he could or not. My wages were certainly garnished!

After the incident was paid off, I transferred to a different district, where I drove for elementary school students. They were more well-behaved than high school and junior high school students. I loved those little people. Every Friday, I'd have some bags of chips and candy to give them; they got to choose which one they wanted, but they could not have both. Some of the parents appreciated the extra care that I showed their children, and others were just plain miserable. The appreciative parents would have their children bring me little gifts for Christmas, and I felt so appreciated. I didn't like driving the school bus, but I did what I needed to do to not live inside my parents' home any longer.

I was 19 years old when I had finally had enough. I knew that I no longer wanted to live in the same house as my absent father. He was too mean and unapologetic, and he always felt that everything had to be done his way. He still spoke to me disrespectfully—it was obvious that he was still trying to belittle me—but I was starting to see that I didn't have to continue giving my power to a bully. I saved up two paychecks from driving the bus and moved into a duplex on the Westside of town, in a neighborhood called Creektown. I lived on what the community called "the back street." Its name, though, was Prince Street. The row of duplexes looked shabby and unkept, from the top of the street, so one would easily assume that we had roaches and rats running wild through our homes. Truth is, we kept our places clean, and we did not experience problems with rodents.

My duplex was a small two-bedroom, one bath, and kitchen. Upon entry, you'd be standing in my small living room. While in the living room, the first door to the right was a bedroom that I didn't really have a purpose for, and on the other side of that wall was the second bedroom where I slept. Next to my bedroom was the kitchen, and on the other side of the kitchen wall was the bathroom.

At some point during that year, I decided to enroll in the Universal College of Beauty. It was within walking distance of Johnson C. Smith University (JCSU), an HBCU, Five Points convenience store, Church's Chicken, Chicken King, and the corner gas station, which never had a sign up. Deep down, I had always wanted to attend JCSU, but I didn't know how to get into a *real* college.

After doing a few finger-wave sets, accidentally burning someone's hair with a Marcel iron, and doing Jheri curls, I realized that doing hair was not my thing. So, I dropped out of beauty school. I allowed myself grace. No one gave me a manual that told me how to move forward in life. I told myself that I would start over someday—that starting over did not mean failure and also did not mean that I was too old to start over. What I was too old for was to keep doing the same things that were not working for my good. Starting over meant growth, courage, and the wisdom to change directions when needed.

I had no idea what I wanted to be in life, mostly because I didn't have any professional influence while growing up.

I recall my brother's first wife's brother telling me, "You change jobs more than I change drawers." I thought to myself, *He should change more often*, because I wasn't switching jobs that much.

I did know that I wanted to do something with my life other than working in a restaurant or at a warehouse. I was absolutely certain that I didn't want to have to stand on my feet all day to earn a living. I didn't want to continue driving a school bus either, but knowing that my grade-point average in high school was a nightmare, how could I possibly get into an HBCU—or any other university, for that matter?

I was not a dumb kid; I was lazy and had not had anyone encouraging me to do well in high school.

Neither of my parents had completed high school, so maybe they didn't know to set educational expectations for me. My mother had dropped out of high school when she became pregnant with my brother; my father did not attend school beyond the sixth grade.

The only college influence came from watching TV. One show, *A Different World*, depicted the lives of African American students attending an HBCU—something I desired, but I didn't know who to ask for help. DuckDuckGo and Google didn't exist back then.

Halloween came and went in 1992, and it seemed like Thanksgiving wasn't wasting time making its presence known. I called my mom and asked her to talk me through making a sweet potato pie, and she said she would as long as I made one for her, too. She told me the ingredients I'd need, and off to the store I went, to purchase the items.

During this time in my life, the Charlotte Area Transit System was my mode of transportation. So, I carefully planned how to get the pie to my parents without breaking the crust, or worse, dropping the entire pie.

Considering the buses were running on a holiday schedule, I decided to get to my parents' home as early as possible.

I was happy to see my mom, and even happier that my father was not at home.

Thank God! I did not want to deal with his cruel remarks.

When my father phoned home and told my mom he was on his way back to the house, I took that as my cue to leave.

As I said earlier, my father was so mean to me when I was growing up. He would belittle me and was verbally abusive. He spoke negatively anytime he had something to say to me. He was always criticizing anything I did, no matter what it was. And he beat me; the last time was when I was 12.

I didn't want to see him, so I left before he got back home.

When I got home, I called my mother to let her know that I had made it back home, and told her I'd see her next week.

When I went to visit her the following week, the pie was still in their refrigerator, uncut. I was offended, to say the least. When I asked my mom why they hadn't eaten it, she said to me, "Your daddy said you might've put something in it to kill him!" I still remember that, even though it happened over three decades ago! Like, who TF thinks like that?

My father always felt like I'd do something to retaliate, but the Word says: "Vengeance is mine. I will repay, says the Lord." What my father said and did wasn't normal, wasn't loving, and wasn't something a child could ever deserve. With that sweet potato pie, I had been a young woman trying to offer something kind, something homemade, something made by my own hands… and he projected his own guilt, paranoia, and cruelty onto me. After all the beatings, belittling, and emotional chaos I'd endured, I'd still taken a homemade pie across town on a bus to honor my parents on Thanksgiving Day. I showed up with generosity, even when it wasn't given back.

I had to learn that my father's reaction to the pie wasn't about me. It was about the guilt he carried, the kind that twists love into suspicion, kindness into threat. People who expect retaliation often do so because they know they deserve it. I wasn't the danger. His conscience was. That pattern, the mistrust, the paranoia—none of it came from anything I had done. It came from *everything* he had not faced.

I left their home after that follow-up visit with my sweet potato pie. I was almost in tears when I told my mom, "You know that I would never do anything to hurt y'all. I will call you when I get home." I cried a little bit on the bus ride back to my place. It disturbed me to know that my own mother could be influenced to believe that I would have been capable of poisoning them.

When I got home, I made sure my attitude was in check, and that I didn't sound like I was crying. I called her—my name and number showed up on the caller ID box—but my father picked up the phone anyway. I heard him when he said hello, but I said, "Hey, Ma. I just called to let you know that I made it home." I hung the phone up right after saying that, because I did not want to hear his voice.

Maybe 10 minutes after I had hung up the phone on my father, my phone rang. I didn't recognize the number, but I answered anyway. The voice on the other end said, "Hey, Angie. How you doing?" I immediately knew that it was my cousin Kizzie, and I was so happy to hear her voice! Kizzie was tall and very slender, beautiful dark skin, and an awesome smile.

In an excited pitch, I said, "Hey, Kizzie! I am good. How are you?"

"I am good," she said. "I just wanted to call and see how you was doing. And to find out if I could come stay with you."

I didn't give it a second thought when I told her, "Absolutely! Are you leaving your grandma's house?"

"No," she said. "You know, Angie, me and Marvetta were placed in group homes." Marvetta was her younger sister. Marvetta had a dimple in her chin like our grandmother, and her complexion was caramel brown, she's about the same height as her sister, and was the average sized teenager. I looked around my place like, *WTF?* I told her that I did not know that had happened to them. She let me know that she would speak with her social worker and that she'd be in touch with me.

Well, the day came when I met the social worker. Kizzie was there too. The social worker came to my duplex to do an assessment, and she asked me how old I was. I told her that I was 19 and that my 20th birthday would be the following year in August. The social worker told me that she wished she met with more families who were like me, that were willing to take their family members in, to keep them out of the system.

"You are very mature for your age," she told me. "You have steady employment, and your place is tidy. Unfortunately, the State of North Carolina requires a guardian to be 21 years old."

I don't know if I started crying before my cousin or not, but I said to the social worker, "So, you're saying my cousin cannot live with me?"

"By law, I am not at liberty to assign guardianship to you," she said.

I told my cousin that I was sorry I failed her, but that I'd tried. We hugged for a minute, and the social worker said she was going to go to her car to give us a minute. When I saw her sitting in the Department of Social Services vehicle, I told my cousin to hold on for one moment. I went to my room and got two quarters and a dime; back then, it cost only sixty cents to ride the city bus. I told my cousin to take that money and, after getting out of school the next day, run away and come to my house.

I made that decision because my auntie, Kizzie's mother, had given up a baby girl for adoption, maybe four or five years prior. When the baby girl was born, my auntie allowed me to name her. I chose the name Brittany Trinae Leak, but I don't think it mattered, because the adoptive parents had the legal right to change her name. I understood that adoption meant I would never get to know that tiny little person that I had the honor of naming. I did not know what a foster home was at the time, though.

Kizzie explained to me the experience she'd faced with regards to how she ended up in a group home. I became so infuriated! My protective instinct grew stronger. I can't explain it, but I felt a strong sense of responsibility to my family. Even though I was very young and unsupported, I had the capacity to act like the person I needed someone to be for me.

When Kizzie caught the bus and arrived at my place the next day, she asked me if her sister could come live with us, and I told her yes! I didn't want either of them to be separated from family any longer.

My heart was so full when the both of them were finally back together under the same roof.

After they'd been living with me for a while, Marvetta told me that she saw me as a mother figure. I was blown away, because I just felt like I was being "big cuz" looking out for my family.

On my 21st birthday, I got into a physical altercation with my sister. She'd called me and asked if she could stay a couple of nights because she didn't have any place to sleep. I felt compelled to help her and told her yes, she could come for a few nights.

I learned that day how much drugs had taken a toll on her overall being. She was so hostile toward our cousins and kept trying to fight them. I told her she had to leave, to which she replied, "I ain't going no-damn-where!"

I said, "Well, 911 will be called because I'm not putting up with your foolishness."

With her whole chest, she said, "Call the motherfuckers and see what they tell your dumb ass! I ain't got to go no-damn-where, and they're going to tell you the same shit. Bitch!"

The next thing I know, she came out of my kitchen with a pan of hot grease, thinking she was going to throw it on me. I opened my hand wide and gripped her face before I grabbed her by her throat, got the pan of grease, and told one of my cousins to put it on the stove and to make sure the burners were turned off. I never took my steady hand from her neck! She was very shifty, and I kept up with her. I got her in a chokehold, with both of her hands trapped under one of my arms. She was trying to wrestle to get free.

I told Marvetta to call the police, and when the cops arrived, I still had Tonya in a chokehold. That fine-ass officer asked me to explain what happened, and I told him. I also told him that I wanted her removed from my place. To which the officer said, "Ma'am, this is a domestic situation. You'd have to file an eviction notice with the sheriff's office to have her removed."

I looked at that officer and told him, "I tell you what. You can take her with you now, or it's a guarantee that you'll be back tonight. And when you come back, one of us will be leaving out of here on a stretcher, and it won't be me!"

The officer looked at my sister and asked her, "Do you have your things together? Let's go. You have to leave the premises."

She called me every type of bitch that she could think of, stole my canned goods, and tried to spit on me as she walked out the door. The officer told her he was placing her under arrest for assault. That was the night I learned that spitting in the direction of someone is considered an assault.

That night, I smoked my very first cigarette. A Newport.

People claim that time heals old wounds. The following year, during Christmas break from Charlotte Mecklenburg Schools (CMS) my sister called and asked if she could come spend the night with me. Without dwelling on the past, I told her she could. I showed her the wrapped gifts that I'd gotten from the children on my school bus route, and she asked what the other presents were for. My first thought was to tell her that they were just empty boxes, but I was honest and let her know that I'd gotten our cousin Tavares the Ninja Turtle figure he wanted for Christmas, and I'd gotten his sister, Quinetta, the doll she'd asked for. Quinetta and Tavares lost their mother when they were very young; she was three years old, and he was still a newborn. Their mom was my mother's younger sister, and in 1984 after their mother passed, Quinetta (we often called her Netta) grew up calling my mother "Mama," too.

Well, based on what she did next, apparently my sister was still carrying the anger wound from the night she'd gotten arrested the previous year for acting like a country-ass monkey in my duplex. I thought we were good. I let her know that I was going to be leaving for a little while, to take my nephew and niece their gifts.

I thought I could trust her.

When I was at my nephew and niece's house, my sister called.

"Hello?" I said. "You miss me? Is that why you're calling?"

She sounded so calm and relaxed, saying, "Angie, somebody broke into your apartment and took the gifts from under your Christmas tree."

I was stunned. Out of all the years I'd lived in that duplex, no one had ever broken into my place! My brother asked me how she'd sounded on the phone when she told me, and then said, "She is high as hell. Ain't nobody break into your apartment. She sold your shit to the dope man!"

I caught the bus back home, and she was gone by the time I got there. My neighbor at the time who lived to the left of me told me, "Angie. Ain't nobody break into your place. Your sister wanted to keep getting high and said she knew where she could get some shit from. And that's when she came out of the house with a garbage bag filled with wrapped presents."

I'd been hurt by my sister's actions yet again. She was literally the Grinch that stole Christmas!

***

A few years later, just before I turned 23, I met my six-foot teddy bear.

Here's how and why we met. One of my cousins from my father's side of the family was my neighbor in Creektown, and one night, she knocked on my door and asked if I'd go out with her sister-in-law, Ann. My cousin said she wasn't feeling well, and she had to go to work the next morning.

I didn't want to go out that night either. I was at home alone for the first time in a while, and I wanted to enjoy watching TV. But my cousin was adamant about my going, so I agreed. I told her to give me some time to have a bath and get dressed.

Meanwhile, I informed Shavon Harrison (now Shavon Land), who was like the little sister I never had and lived on the other side of me, to look out over my place while I would be away for a little while.

I put on my black jeans with a satin purple top and black knee-high boots, and put some soft curls in my hair. I was only trying to look presentable and wasn't expecting to meet anyone that night.

Ann and I got to a club called Trails of Thunder. It was loud. Motorcycles were everywhere outside. We stayed long enough to feel that the timing was off for a girl's night out, especially since we didn't know each other that well.

Just as we were about to leave, we heard someone trying to get our attention. I assumed they were calling for Ann, so I went to the edge of the street to give them privacy to talk.

When I turned around, the man was approaching me. He reminded me so much of the singer-songwriter Gerald Levert—the beard, the complexion, the vibe. He was six-feet tall, dark complexion, solid build, and a mischievous smile. He introduced himself and asked for my name. I was a skeptic, so I didn't tell him my real name. I told him my name was Lady.

He said he had to go pick someone up, and asked me to ride with him.

My face had to be saying what my words were not, because *Mr. Six-Foot Teddy Bear Sir Man, I just met you! I ain't getting in a car with a complete stranger. Especially after something unfortunate happened to me at 15.*

I declined the ride-along, and he told me, "Alright. Well, stay here until I get back." I told him that I wasn't driving, and he turned to Ann and said, "Pardon me, Miss. Would you make sure she's here when I get back? I'm just going down the road a lil ways, and I'll be right back. I promise."

I watched as he went and got in his car, and I looked at Ann and said, "Let's go."

Ann was such a nice person, and she nicely told me, "He might be a really good guy. Give him a chance. Don't run out on him."

I just looked at her and thought how much I'd rather be at home watching TV.

Upon his return, we exchanged phone numbers.

Our first date was at a diner called Rock-Ola Cafe. I felt awkward because it was my first real date. Like, ever! My Six-Foot Teddy Bear showed up with a bouquet of flowers, and it blew my mind. I was so inexperienced. Afterward, he took me to meet his dad, which made me a little uncomfortable because I didn't know I needed to meet the parents. I was so naïve.

He became my first boyfriend. Later on, his mother found out that I met his dad before I met her, and *oh my gawd!*

Her name was Mary, but everyone lovingly called her Mae. I said, "Hello, Miss Mae."

She said, "Ain't no… Miss Mae, my ass! Call me Mae!"

From that day on, I felt like I was a part of his family.

Each year that we were together, I went with him to family gatherings for Thanksgiving and Christmas. His family gatherings did not feel like a chore, or like he was asking too much for me to be there. I enjoyed the unity of family. The bonding. Something that I longed for in my own family. Christmas music would be playing during December. Not one person had to shoo children away, because the kids already understood the assignment (exit the room where all adults are present). We set up the tables to play games of Spades. I kept offering to help Mae to finish setting up the food tables, but she told me to go enjoy the Spades game. There was plenty of ganja to smoke, runs were already completed to the liquor store, and there were coolers filled with sodas, bottled water, and beer. The aroma of chicken frying was lovely! Before meeting my six-foot teddy bear, I thought large family gatherings occurred only in Christmas movies. There was so much love shown between everyone, and it was genuine.

He introduced me to his brothers and his friends, and whenever they saw me out at the club without him, they referred to me as his girl and basically blocked any dudes from approaching me.

My teddy bear and I eventually decided that I would give up my apartment and move in with him. Kizzie and Marvetta were already living in different places, and they were safe. My teddy bear and I would lie in bed side by side, night after night, without intimacy. By the second month and still no pancaking, I was wondering if he was even attracted to me, because the subject of intercourse never came up. I was feeling mighty frisky. I decided to write him a note that said, "Would you like to have sex?" I included a box for yes or no, and the note instructed him, "Check one of these boxes."

He checked "yes." I had never experienced a climax before, and the fact that I experienced the first with him made me fall much deeper in love. I loved everything about that man.

My family, namely my grandfather, did not appreciate the fact that

I was unmarried and living with a man. As an adult, I talked on the phone with my grandfather daily. And each time, he'd ask me if I was still shacking up. I hated that term, but I wasn't going to disrespect him either.

The weekend before Christmas in 1995, I had spoken with my grandpa several times, and each time we got off the phone, I would say to him, "Goodbye." He would correct me and say, "'Goodbye' means forever. So, I will talk to you later, young lady."

In the wee hours of the of Christmas morning, I woke up, because my chest felt heavy. My teddy bear was hanging out with his friends, so I was at home alone. I drank a cup of ice-cold water, thinking it would help with my breathing. It didn't. I couldn't get back to sleep, no matter how much I tried. I turned on the TV and watched *In the Heat of the Night* until a different show came on.

Later on that morning, my mother called and said, "Come and get Daddy's house key and go check on him for me please. Aunt Sarah said she knocked on his door but didn't get an answer."

I woke up my teddy bear and told him what my mom had asked of me, and we went to get the key. I told him that my grandfather was in his place dead.

"You don't know that," he said. "Think positive."

We got to my grandfather's place. The screen door was locked. I knocked on the door so loudly that neighbors peeped out the door to see what the matter was. I asked one of his neighbors to call the police.

I swear, it felt like they arrived in two seconds flat! I recognized one of the officers as Rambo—that was the name he'd earned on the streets of Charlotte. He was ready to snatch the screen door off the hinges, but I stopped him. I told him there was a tear in the screen, and that he could use a little twig to unlatch the lock, and I handed him the door key.

Rambo told me, "Stay right here, ma'am."

"I want to go inside too!" I said.

"We have to secure the area and make sure it's safe," he insisted.

Rambo and the other officers entered my grandfather's duplex. When they returned, Rambo said to me, "I'm sorry, ma'am, but he's gone."

Not ready to accept the reality, I said, "Gone where? The front and back screen doors were locked; the windows aren't open. What do you mean 'gone'?"

He placed his heavy hand on my shoulder and gently said, "He passed away."

I let out a bloodcurdling scream.

I cried so hard and said, "That's why he said goodbye to me when we got off the phone last night. He knew that his goodbye was forever."

I couldn't think of what to do next. In fact, I don't even know what I did.

The day of the funeral, what hurt me even more was the fact that my teddy bear didn't go with me… he didn't say why he'd chosen not to attend, he just said he wasn't going.

I needed his support.

I called my six-foot teddy bear Pooh, because he honestly reminded me of Winnie the Pooh. Not in a childish way, but in a way that I knew he was big enough to protect me and soft enough to comfort me. He made me feel safe—he protected me in ways that I previously had never known existed.

I felt loved.

I was *in* love.

Somewhere around the two-and-a-half-year mark of our relationship, sadly, he started putting his friends and desire to do music before me. I felt like he put me on the back burner to simmer.

I said something to him about it, and being the gentleman that he was, he took me out on a date to a mini golf place. I was pleased because he gave me a date night, and it felt like we were getting "us" back. After we left there, we stopped by Blockbuster to rent a video. I wasn't a fan of horror movies, but we got one of those Chucky movies and some other movies to watch.

Things seemed to be going great for a while, but he fell back into his old habit of putting friends and music first. I got tired of sitting in the house alone with no transportation and nothing to do. One night, an associate I'd gone to high school with called me and asked if I wanted to go to Club Utopia. I had never heard of the spot, but she knew that it was a joint that hosted all-male revues. The decision was an easy one to make, because I figured if I wasn't going to spend time with my teddy bear, and he was out having fun, then I might as well do the same.

I was disgusted with constantly trying to find my place in our relationship. I didn't want to sound like a broken record, and I knew I didn't like being on the back burner yet again! That night, I met a mysterious man. I was no longer being ignored; that man changed the simmer to a rapid boil. I am by no means proud of what I did—I was unfaithful. I had a fling, and I'm not making excuses, but my teddy bear had emotionally abandoned me. I didn't feel seen. I didn't feel needed. But I did feel awful about what I'd done.

I had to confess my sins to someone, and thought I could trust my sister. She loved my teddy bear like he was her real brother and immediately told me that she was going to tell him. I learned that day not to trust her with any secrets. He was at work, and I had time to think about what to tell him. Being that my sister's addiction had caused her to steal from us before, I told him that she was trying to blackmail me to get some money out of me. I lied and said, "She told me that she was going to tell you I cheated on you if I didn't give her some money."

"What type of sister does that?" he asked me.

I let out a silent sigh of relief, but I felt guilty as hell. I'd cheated and lied to my teddy bear. I carried that guilt around for months before I finally confessed. We spoke like respectful adults, and I apologized.

"As long as you didn't get pregnant by them," he said. He accepted my apology and never threw it up in my face. Ever.

I went back to the Universal College of Beauty, briefly. My teddy bear believed in my hairstyling capabilities and had a great idea to capitalize on in the hair industry, but I knew that I didn't want to do hair. My heart was simply not into it.

And eventually, my heart was no longer into him.

Even though we had broken up for a little while, all together, we gave five years to our relationship. I feel like we were each other's placeholder, in that we never said "I do." So, at that point, weren't we placeholders wasting each other's time? I thought I wanted to be married, but he was not "the one."

I remained cordial with him, because he was a solid dude, and if I needed to talk as a friend, he listened.

After our breakup, I was still trying to fulfill my desire of getting a college education. I saw a lot of television ads about Brookstone College of Business, so I enrolled in its business management program. I was a night student, because I drove as a paraprofessional driver for the Department of Social Services during the day, but I was ecstatic because I was finally enrolled in college!

I was in a place where I never thought I'd be.

The seed my father had tried to plant when he said I'd never be shit did not take root.

But just as I thought, *I'll show him*, I sadly found myself losing interest in the program, and dropped out of night school.

I started partying every weekend.

During the summer months of the '90s, you could easily find a lot of young adults hanging out at Hornet's Nest Park, the carwash on North Tryon Street, or along Beatties Ford Road.

One night, Orviece (I called her Vee) and I were leaving the park, but I needed to stop and get gas for my Geo Storm. Vee and I went to high school together, we lost contact, and when we saw one another again, we remained in contact. She was close to me like a sister. Vee reminded me so much of Chaka Khan, her smile was magnetic. She was beautiful just like Chaka Khan, she resembled the younger version of Chaka.

Since it was very hot and humid that day, I had on a blue-and-yellow floral jumper. It looked like a minidress, but really the bottom was shorts.

My hair was in box braids that were curled on the ends. Part of the braids were up in a ponytail, with the rest of them down. I had on white sandals and lotion in a scent called Sun Ripened Raspberry from Bath & Body Works.

I got out of my car at the gas station and proceeded to the entrance of the store to go inside and get some things. A man with a motorcycle held the door for me to go inside, and I thanked him.

After I paid for my items and walked out of the store, this very tall (maybe 6'3"), very dark chocolate, and less attractive dude, got off of his motorcycle and followed me to my car.

We exchanged numbers.

As I was driving my Geo Storm out of the parking lot—with the volume loud, like I had bass, even though I had no bass, all treble—Vee said, "You're out here mesmerizing dudes. Ass just bouncing." In between laughs, she moved her hands to imitate the movement of my booty. She was laughing so hard but still managed to say, "He followed you to your car. Like Smokey and Craig said in *Friday*, daaaaam-mmnn!" We had already puffed and passed, so maybe we were just high, or she was hella funny.

That man on the motor cycle became my rebound. My summer fling. We were not in a relationship, because he was already with some-one and I had just gotten out of a relationship, so the setup was fine for that time.

I don't know what he told his girlfriend to get out of the house, but we were at the Marriott and Holiday Inn a lot! The first time we were intimate, he said, "I have to let you know that I have a small penis. So please don't pick on me."

I giggled like a schoolgirl. I had never had a man tell me anything of the sort.

He was not truthful. Mr. Motorcycle Man was pleasantly well-en-dowed!

He told me that his girlfriend worked at the Bi-Lo grocery store. My associate from high school that I had gone to Club Utopia with, for the all-male revue, went to the store with me. At some point, my associate referred to me as her best friend, but she didn't behave as a best friend. She would change her number, disappear, and suddenly re-appear—that wasn't best friend behavior in my opinion. It wasn't even *friend* behavior.

I just wanted to see what the girlfriend looked like.

I asked for her by name, saying that someone had told me she'd done their microbraids, and I was looking for someone to do mine. She assured me that she was the only person at that store location with her name. Before I left the store I asked her if the motor cycle man, I'd been having a fling with was her boyfriend.

She said, "Yeah! How do you know?" She looked like she saw fire and was ready to rage. "Okay. Who are you?" she asked.

I told her, "I am the reason he's telling you he's going to work, but he's really with me. My number is on your caller ID. Call me if you want to chat."

My associate and I left the store.

The next day, I expected Mr. Motorcycle Man to be upset and rais-ing hell. This joker told me, "Thank you! You did me a favor, because I was ready for her to leave."

I was cool with things the way they were, he was my rebound, and not really my type. He was fresh out of a relationship and he wanted to see other people, so we agreed to chill and not see one another so often, until we finally just stopped altogether.

# The Man Who Once Lived in Panama

In 2001, I accepted a job as a special transportation driver with the City of Charlotte. I loved the fact that my schedule was initially Monday through Friday, which meant my weekends were free for me to enjoy life. Which is how I ended up at the R&B Lounge on North Tryon Street.

One night at the R&B Lounge, I met a man who'd once lived in Panama. He was old enough to be my father, but he didn't look very old—except the fact that he was missing his two front teeth. He had brown eyes that seemed a bit larger than the normal sized eyeballs (his eyes were what some people would call being "popeyed"). We were about the same height… he was maybe 160 with a little beer belly, and seemed to have the manners of a real southern gentleman. Sadly, no one had ever sat me down and told me the ins and outs of relationships, and I still didn't know my value back then. I dated this man. He was just three years younger than my mother.

I began spending a significant amount of time with Mr. Panama Man, and one day, he asked me if I would like to ride with him up to New York to take his son back home. I had to get time off work, but being that it was during our busiest season, I probably wouldn't have gotten the time off if I'd said the real reason. I told my supervisor that I was going to attend a funeral in New York, and that I wasn't going to miss my auntie's services. I knew no one in New York. The company's requirement was that I bring back an obituary. That was weird, but okay, their rule. Mr. Panama Man told me that we could stop by one of the funeral parlors to get an obituary. And when we did, we had to ring the doorbell to get inside. Why?

"This is your first time to New York, so you don't know, but people black-market organs," he said. A funeral parlor selling people's organs! I was so shocked I couldn't speak.

After we returned from New York, we signed a lease on an apartment in Double Oaks together, and he took me to Atlanta for my birthday. It was his first time going to Atlanta. He was so ecstatic, and it was such a delightful trip.

He'd called ahead to the Hilton, where we were staying, and had sunflowers and yellow roses in the room waiting for me. He'd remembered my telling him that sunflowers were my favorite flower!

We went to the Martin Luther King, Jr. Historical Park, Zoo Atlanta, an adult novelty shop, the Underground, and the Coca-Cola museum.

A few staff members incorrectly identified me as his daughter. I didn't have to utter a word, because in his moments of chivalry, he corrected them politely with a smile on his face.

He wanted to find some ganja while we were there, and it just so happened that there was a "florist" in the parking lot of the Kmart. The neighborhood we were in did not look friendly at all. I could only imagine what it looked like at night.

I was so nervous, I turned down a one-way street into oncoming traffic! But we didn't crash into anything.

When we returned to our apartment, I told him that I was going out with my cousins later that night. I was honest and let him know that we'd be going to The Jam; it was a club down in Rock Hill, South Carolina, and it was literally in a trailer! He wasn't able to go because he had to work, so my cousins Vern and Dwayne (were brother and sister), plus Dwayne's wife and some of their friends went with me to keep celebrating my birthday. Vern was always ready for a good time, she and I used to go to clubs together in the late 90s. Vern is on the shorter side, even though she doesn't like to admit it. She was dark skinned and was more on the petite side. Dwayne, her youngest brother was tall like their father, caramel complexion like their mother, and an all-around handsome guy. His wife (Sabrina) was beauty pageant type of beautiful, but she wasn't arrogant, and that's what enhanced her beauty even more. One of my associates from the neighborhood rode with me, and she had her Mary Jane with her. I had on a white pantsuit, not just any old regular suit. The pants were pleated from waist to ankle, and they were sheer and free-flowing bell bottoms. The jacket was long enough to cover enough below my waistline. I had on a lime green hat with matching earrings, and it just so happened that I'd found some lime green sandals. I was comfortable and I felt cute.

I was feeling pretty good when we left. But the road I had to drive on to get to I-77 was so dark, I started low-key panicking. My associate from my neighborhood, who was riding in the car with me, asked if I wanted her to fire up the joint, and I told her to wait until we crossed the North Carolina state line.

All of a sudden, I saw blue lights in my rearview mirror, followed by the sound of a siren!

The cop walked up to my car, and when he spoke, his voice had the most country twang I'd ever heard! He asked me if I knew why he'd stopped me.

"I don't know," I said. "I'm just trying to get to 77 northbound."

He didn't care what I was talking about, because he kept writing.

He handed me a speeding ticket—a 50-dollar ticket on my birthday!

He told me that I didn't have to appear in court, but I would need to mail the payment to the PO box listed on the ticket, and to make it out to his name. I thought that was sketchy, but he said he was cutting me some slack because I had a commercial driver's license and it was my burfdae (I swear that was how it sounded). When I got home, I told Mr. Panama Man what had happened. He gave me the 50 bucks and told me to go get a money order to pay the fine.

He made sure I was taken care of. I wanted for nothing. Anytime I stopped for gas, he'd pay and pump. He said to me, "What I look like, as a man, if I can't pump gas in the car for my woman?" He made sure

I had lunch money. I was spoiled a little bit. On our date nights, we always got out of the house. He wanted to go to the movies and dinner or to go shoot pool. But not the club where we'd met. He told me, "I cain't take you back to where I met you." He says it was because another dude was pushing up on me. I knew exactly what he was talking about, but I told Mr. Panama Man that I didn't remember it, and honestly, that guy wasn't important to me. I knew how to feed his ego.

He wasn't what I'd call a romantic, but he had an idea for how to set the mood.

The first time we made love, I was much like in the lyrics from Betty Wright's song "Tonight Is the Night." More specifically, the part where she sang, "I'm nervous and I'm trembling' / Waitin' for you to walk in / I'm tryin' hard to relax / But I just can't keep still."

The boom box was on WPEG's Quiet Storm, and LSG's "My Body" had just gone off.

We'd just finished puffing and passing. Ganja is a natural aphrodisiac for me, but I needed something to calm me down too.

Just then, I said to myself, *All of our dates, talks, laughs, and walks while holding hands have led up to this moment; no turning back now.*

The next song on the radio was Ginuwine's "Pony."

My heart started racing when his lips connected with mine.

And since my knees were good and would dare not betray me, I got on top.

I was moist and in control, so I allowed him to enter with ease.

My motions matched the rhythm of the song. He was my pony, and I was damn sure gonna ride. He growled and said, "Damn, Annnggie! Shhhhhhhit." The sounds of wetness were on a different level.

I paused on the part of the song where Ginuwine sings, "If we're gonna get nasty baby / First we'll show and tell."

He looked me in my eyes.

I didn't say a word.

I stayed on top.

Motionless.

The only things moving were the muscles of my vaginal walls.

I teased him as I squeezed him. Then I relaxed the muscles, and I repeated this until I heard him moan and let out a long, "Oooooh shit! Angie! Girl!"

He gripped me by my waist and laid me on my back.

With one hand, he held onto my brown round bottom.

I could feel his heart racing.

Aaliyah's "Rock the Boat" was the only other sounds I heard.

Once he was fully inside me, I wrapped my long legs around his back, and he thoroughly worked the middle.

Our moans matched.

His strokes were masterful. He. Made. Love. To. Me!

I cried out his name… he slowed his strokes, but he had no intention of stopping. Neither did I want him to.

I got back on top for maybe 60 seconds, and just then, we both trembled as we reached a powerful climax.

His body jerked. My legs trembled.

We lay there with my head on his chest, and his arm caressing me, and I felt so satisfied.

The next day, we attended a cookout at the home of one of his relatives.

He introduced me to his family, and when I met his sister, she let it be known that she did not like me. He, along with others, said to overlook her because she would run off at the mouth like that at everybody.

***

A few months had passed before I'd learned that Mr. Panama Man had lied to me. He'd told me that he had never been married, when in fact, he had gotten married when he was in the military, while stationed in Panama.

And he was *still married*! His wife was living in New York. Not only that, but he was fooling around with one of his coworkers!

I was *The First 48* type of hot!

Granted, he was *very* well-endowed, but that didn't mean he needed to go sharing it like it was a bag of Halloween candy.

The same week that I found out he was married and his wife was living in New York state, is the same week that I learned he was cheating on me with his coworker.

Oh! I failed to mention that the week began with him proposing to me.

The day after I learned of his affair with his coworker, he called me from his job on his lunch break. I am not a bakery, so I didn't sugarcoat anything. He could hear in my tone that something was wrong when I asked him if he was coming home, because that's what he would normally do on his breaks. He said he wasn't coming home, and that the reason he'd left New York was so that he didn't have to worry about sleeping with one eye open. That thoroughly pissed me off!

Cheating on me while we were actively living under the same roof was absurd. Absolutely insane! We shared a bed, for heaven's sake! We shared the same bathroom, dinner table, private moments, and life's stressors, and yet he still found time to sneak into someone else's arms and bed. Then had the audacity to crawl back into our sheets, which smelled like me, the person who trusted him the most.

His choices did not equal confusion. It was a calculated decision, because he took drastic measures to plan it all out, hide it, and lie about it, and then looked me square in my eyes daily!

Pretending everything was normal.

He ate my food, and I mean, all of the countless meals I prepared.

He accepted my love, comfort, support, and loyalty while actively betraying me.

I realized that was a different level of selfishness, because if he was unhappy, he could have sat down with me and talked. Instead, he chose ego over accountability, and the craziest part was how he *expected* forgiveness.

He understood fully the damage he'd caused, and I reminded him that he had zero regard for my emotional stability.

Perhaps this was karma showing up to exact revenge from what I'd done to my six-foot teddy bear. He'd been my first boyfriend, as I said. I mean, I'd known guys, but I had not been intimate with them. I didn't know how to be a girlfriend, and I'm sure I messed up a lot of things. I just hope that he has forgiven the younger, inexperienced me.

And as for Mr. Panama Man, it didn't really dawn on me until after the fact why he would wear my Pearberry lotion from Bath & Body Works. It was because she wore the same fragrance.

The first time I saw him putting on my lotion, I was confused. I thought he had something he needed to tell me. It had to have shown on my face, because he said, "I will buy you some more lotion, Angie!"

I looked into his muddy brown eyes and said to him, "I am not concerned about you buying me more lotion. Do you have something you want to tell me?"

He immediately said, "I ain't gay, if that's what you're trying to say, Angie!" I cackled. That was a mischievous moment on his behalf. He knew what he was doing, I didn't. He was masking her scent. I just shook my head and laughed.

I had to go to the doctor the next day, because it had been a while since I'd had a bowel movement. I started losing weight, large ring-worm-looking spots started popping up on my arms and legs, and the backs of my calves looked like I was having an allergic reaction to something.

I knew that I was allergic to Tide washing powder, and thought maybe that was what had stirred up this mysterious illness. And that's what I told people about my skin when they'd ask.

Anytime I'd touch a strand of hair, I'd get a headache. I started having nose bleeds, my breathing was choppy, and my vision was very blurry.

I'd already seen different specialists, trying to determine what illness had plagued me. I was hoping a new doctor, Iris Cheng, could tell me what the matter was. I got undressed and put on one of the fashionable gowns they give to patients, and waited for the doctor to enter the room. I was so nervous. I was alone at the appointment, which seemed to be a reflection of my life: alone when I really needed support.

Dr. Cheng told me, "You have sarcoidosis. It is common among African American women."

I checked out, because I got sick of hearing that damn near every disease known to man was common among Black people.

I had to have X-rays done on my chest and ankles, because the disease was causing breathing trouble and arthritic pain in my joints.

When the radiologist showed me the black blotches on my lungs, I was petrified. I thought I was being handed my death sentence!

I went to my parents' home after I left that appointment, and talked to my mother about my diagnosis. Mrs. Jackson was there, and she was so concerned for me. She told me to make sure I kept all of my appointments. I knew that she was saying it with love.

I felt that.

I did not know that a registered nurse was scheduled to visit with my mom on that day, and that she'd come into the house while I was smoking a cigarette and telling Mama and Mrs. Jackson about the sarcoidosis. The nurse stopped in her tracks and said to me, "How are you doing, young lady?"

I looked up at her and told her I was okay, but I was experiencing different pains.

She said, "Did I just hear you correctly? Did you say you have sarcoidosis?"

I thought she was about to drop some wisdom, and I answered, "Yes. I went to different doctors over the past couple of months trying to find out what was happening to me."

The nurse did not sugarcoat a thing. She said, "You have sarcoidosis, and you're smoking! Cigarettes by themselves can kill you. And you have a lung disease that could cause you death due to the fact that you are smoking!"

Anyone who has tried to quit smoking cigarettes knows how hard it is to quit. That wasn't my wake-up call, though. I put my Newport out until she left, then I lit it back up. Defiant.

When I went to my place to deal with the drama that had unfolded, I called the person who'd given themselves the title of being my best friend, because she was available at the time. I asked her to come and help me to move my things out of the apartment. I had just gone to Winn-Dixie and bought some groceries; I had also just finished paying the utilities. The boom box was playing Ginuwine's "Pony," and I thought of Mr. Panama Man. It's funny how songs can trigger my memory. Not funny ha-ha, but that's how memory works when something matters.

Music is basically emotional Velcro.

What's wild is that songs don't bring back *facts*—they bring back truth.

The emotional truth.

The sensory truth.

I continued packing and removed all of my food from the cabinets and the refrigerator.

I called Duke Energy, Piedmont Natural Gas, Southern Bell, and Time Warner Cable to have everything disconnected. The refunds for the monies I had just paid to the utility companies were to be sent to my parents' home.

I removed Mr. Panama Man's clothes from the closets, and with a razor, I cut the inseams from the left legs of all of his jeans and slacks, all the way over to the right sides and down to the cuffs. So, when he held up his pants, they would look like a very long skirt that had not been sewn together properly.

He was very much into name-brand clothes, and I was very much into disrupting his life!

Hurt people hurt people.

I cut the tongues out of all of his left sneakers, and I cut the shoe-strings out of the right sneakers. I put every one of his shirts into the bathtub and poured Clorox on top. When I got tired, I took a permanent black marker and wrote on the bathroom mirror and the walls! I cut up the furniture and then left the door key with our nosy neighbor, Miss Clara.

Mr. Panama Man called my mother like a little wimp and told her what I had done. My mama pleaded with me to not go back over to the apartment, because he promised to have me arrested.

That didn't stop me!

He felt threatened, because in that short amount of time, he had his nephew and his sister move in with him. His sister could have definitely caught all the smoke! His nephew could've gotten these hands, too!

He wouldn't come outside, and that made me madder.

I called my sister and told her what had happened, and she was shocked that I'd had a Bernadine moment—you know, like from *Waiting to Exhale*. Something about the way my sister told me to walk away from the situation and revisit it later saved a window from being broken out—and quite possibly, my first trip to the county jail!

As if I didn't already have enough going on in my life, my mother's baby sister, Shirley Jean, passed away seven days after my birthday, on August 15, 1998.

# The "Experiment"

I moved on from Mr. Panama Man, because there was literally nothing there for us. He'd occasionally page me his code for "I love you," but I wouldn't respond.

I couldn't. He'd betrayed me in the worst way.

Instead, I rekindled the flame I'd had with Mr. Motorcycle Man.

One day, out of the blue, I called him to see how he was doing. I asked if he was in a relationship, because I didn't want to be on the phone with him even on a platonic level if he was with someone else.

We talked about what had gone on between us, and he said he still appreciated my letting his girl know about us, because he was really just ready for her to leave. I asked him why he didn't tell her the truth about how he felt, and he claimed he did, but she wouldn't listen.

He told me he had lost some weight since the last time I'd seen him, and he wanted me to see the new him. I didn't tell him that I had also lost weight, and agreed to see him.

The night I went to his apartment, I had on a sheer black top, a pair of hip-hugging jeans, black platform sandals, and some Midnight Pomegranate lotion from Bath & Body Works.

I knocked at his door, and he opened it.

Without saying a word, he had me in his arms. He said to me, "Damn, girl! You lost some weight, too, I see. You look good! I mean, you looked good before, but look at you! I see you."

We smoked some ganja, an aphrodisiac for me, as I've said.

My rebound was back. He was once again my rebound.

It was late.

The sky was so dark.

He told me he didn't want me outside by myself at night, and insisted that I stay the night with him.

His waterbed stayed moving that night!

The next morning, we showered together, had a session while in the shower, and then I prepared to leave. He wanted me to stay, but I told him I had to go prepare for my mom's Mother's Day cookout, and told him he was welcome to come. He said he wouldn't be able to make it, because he was doing something for his mom and we'd talk later.

He wanted a relationship.

Considering he'd been in a relationship when we met and had no issues cheating on her, I was not about to allow that to happen to me. We called it quits after that. I understood that being wanted feeds the ego, but being valued feeds the soul.

I had gotten approved for a one-bedroom apartment in Shamrock Garden Apartments. The majority of the apartments in the complex were what the leasing office called "garden" units. Upon walking into my apartment, of course you'd be standing in the living room, the kitchen was beside the living room, my bedroom was on the other side of the kitchen's wall, and the bathroom was diagonally across from my bedroom.

Being in this new place was unfamiliar, and I was still eager to go to college.

My schedule changed from Monday through Friday to working every weekend. I hated driving in Charlotte, and I was beginning to feel less satisfied with my job; especially since the supervisor would intentionally assign all of the wheelchair passengers to me. She was always petty and hateful toward me; in turn, I was eager to catch her off of the company's grounds!

It's sad that people who should not be in leadership roles, are often placed there.

One day I had had enough of the supervisor's foolery, and I spoke up in defense of myself. She went to her boss and told her that I needed to be seen by the company's counselor.

The nerve!

A different supervisor had to take me to the counseling appointment, because my hateful supervisor was trying to make it appear as though I was a disgruntled employee. The other goofy-ass supervisor told me I couldn't see my own file, but when I told the counselor about the incident, she handed me the file and allowed me to read it. It was just a bunch of petty bull that I was in no mood for. The counselor figured that out quickly and told me I didn't need any other sessions, but she'd most likely be seeing a lot of my supervisor. I knew it was time for me to leave that job, because the supervisor was delusional and playing around with getting a fresh can of whip-ass opened up on her!

I decided to purchase the *Mavis Beacon Teaches Typing* CD from Walmart. I knew that if I was going to apply for office work, I needed to at least know how to type. In all honesty, the only reason I caught on so quickly was because there was a game as part of the CD; you had to type looking at the computer's screen and beat a chameleon before it made its weird mimicking laugh. I was determined to learn to type!

Once I got my typing up to par, and I knew that I was capable of passing a typing test, I applied for work at some temporary staffing agencies. One of the agencies called me back, and I got a temp job working in human resources at the local Blue Cross Blue Shield (BCBS) office, located in a business park on Nations Ford Road. Around that same time, I met a guy who was a shift supervisor at one of the pizza chains. He was eccentric, to say the least. He was not my type because he was heavier than any man I'd ever dated, but he did have attractive facial features. He was a pecan tanned complexion and about the same height as me. For the sake of not mentioning his name, I refer to him as "the experiment." Our chemistry built up quickly! He tricked me into going to the movies to see *Thirteen Ghosts*, because he told me the movie was comical, but it wasn't. I am not a fan of horror movies, so he ended up having to stay at my place for a week. Of course, I don't think he minded that one bit. His apartment was on the second level, which meant he had to climb stairs, and my apartment was on the ground level.

We didn't do a whole lot of mushy couple stuff, and we were complete opposites. A year after meeting him, I told him that I had a dream that he cheated on me. I really did have a dream that he cheated, and it was so vivid that I can remember the details right now! He looked as though he had swallowed a canary. The fact that the dream was so real and I called him out on what he had done, he thought I was into voodoo or some sort of witchcraft. It makes me laugh just thinking about it. I told him that karma would get him back, and he was certain that I had cast a spell on him!

He would say things to me like, "You got a big nose." Not one time did I tell him that he had an ass that was as wide and flat as the back of my Ford Explorer Sport. He also would read my diary and then talk to me about things that I had never mentioned to him. He would lie about petty stuff, and say that he hadn't been to my apartment on a particular day. To test this theory, I would leave the television on a specific channel, and when I returned home and turned my TV on, it would never be on the channel I had previously watched. He would eat whatever he wanted in the fridge and clean up his mess, as if I wouldn't realize my food was gone. He was doing way too much. Our time was up.

When I broke up with him, he didn't want to return my door key, as if he had rights! I called the leasing office and told them that I'd lost my keys and was afraid that someone would find the key to my apartment and go inside while I was away. Before the end of that day, they'd sent the maintenance worker to my apartment to change the locks. My ex left the door key sitting on one of the bricks that went around the window of the living room.

My time with him was done and I felt that moving 461 miles to Orlando, Florida would put enough space between us. I decided to move to Orlando because I was told that I had a sister who lived there. I had never met her, and I didn't want to spend the rest of my life wondering "what if I had gone to Florida to get to know her and her family?" I took the boldest step I had ever taken in my life.

In 2003, I made a New Year's resolution to quit smoking Newport 100s.

Quitting was one of the hardest things to do, but after my body healed from sarcoidosis, I was diagnosed with asthma. It didn't make much sense to continue smoking, so I quit.

I used vacation time the second week of July to drive down to Florida and get my license changed. Kim, my *sister*, drove me to the DMV office in Orlando to surrender my North Carolina license for a Florida driver's license.

I gave up my Class B CDL, since I knew I would no longer drive a commercial vehicle.

Tonya, my sister, had convinced my parents that I'd be gone for only 30 days, and that they shouldn't worry.

When I returned to Charlotte, I packed all of my clothes from my apartment and loaded them into my Explorer Sport. Then I drove to my parents' home and parked in their carport. My father, ironically, allowed me to drive his Cadillac STS to my "experiment's" apartment. My SUV was packed with everything I owned, so my father insisted I left my vehicle parked there while I went to talk to my ex-experiment. He was still evasive about why he was unfaithful, and I knew we weren't going to be anything beyond what we were, so when I got ready to leave, he literally laid down in front of the door so that I was unable to exit. My body was shaking. *Don't do anything stupid*, I told myself. My adrenaline was on a thousand!

He felt he could explain himself, but what the hell for? The damage had already been done. In that moment, it became very clear to me why he thought I was into witchcraft. I am a seer—it is a gift that I did not ask God for, and at the same time, I'm glad I got it.

I was so hurt. Here I was dealing with the fact that I would be driving for at least eight hours all by myself. Now, I had an ugly breakup to think about as well. That was the longest drive for me, listening to Dru Hill and Brian McKnight on repeat. I didn't have a cell phone at the time, but one of my cousins had made me promise her that I'd go to Family Dollar and purchase a disposable phone. I bought a TracFone when I made it to Orlando.

I safely made it to Kim's home; she allowed me to reside with her until I got my own place. I was there for nearly three months, before moving to my own apartment in Sanford.

I did not know that I had moved to Florida during hurricane season. It rained every day the first week that I was there. I'd look out the window and watch, while the rain hid my tears. I had already accepted a job working for a company that made curtain backdrops for the Olympics and other important events throughout Florida. I worked in human resources as an assistant.

In that job, I met and got involved with someone else's husband. My job took me little time to complete; the supervisor didn't know how to type, so she'd ask me to type up memos and send out emails. I was bored, because what took her all day to do, I could do in 30 minutes flat. Then, the married man kept thinking of stupid reasons to come to HR. Lisa, the receptionist, told me that he was married after she heard him offer to buy my lunch.

"Eating has nothing to do with being married," I told her. "I'm not turning down a free meal!" He was one of the drivers that went to the different locations that did business with the company we worked for. He and another person would set up the curtains for whatever event had been booked, and that was the extent of what I knew in regard to what he actually did in the field.

Perhaps that driver and I became a bit too friendly with each other. He helped me to get over my "experiment." I knew that he was married, but he was also about six foot four, with some of the dreamiest almond eyes, long and curled lashes, naturally curly hair, and a skin tone so bronzed, he could have easily passed for a native Hawaiian. He was a bit on the heftier side, but I wasn't crazy about dudes who were 200 pounds or less.

My decision to become involved with a married man was wild.

I would tell him how uncomfortable I was with deceiving his wife, and he'd say to let him worry about that, or that he was ready to get a divorce from her anyway. I told him, "I hope your divorce has nothing to do with me." And I meant that from the bottom of my heart. I was not about to be with a man who had a baby carrot. Ladies, you know what I mean… but just in case you don't, a baby carrot is slang for referring to a small penis.

Kim took me out for drinks to celebrate my birthday. We went to an Am-Vets, where I had a drink called a blue motorcycle that nearly knocked me flat on my ass! The very next morning, I had a job interview at the insurance company AIG. I was sick of driving 30 minutes to Kissimmee every day to type up memos for a supervisor who typed with one finger! Plus, working somewhere else would lessen how obvious it was that a married man was genuinely interested in me.

So many people told me that they had tried for years to get on with that company but had never received a call back. I guess I was one of the lucky ones, even though I was hungover at my interview. No amount of perfume could mask the smell of alcohol seeping from my pores. I took a shower with my Sun-Ripened Raspberry body gel, and applied the same fragranced lotion, by Bath & Body Works, but somehow that highlighted the smell of alcohol. Perhaps I was paranoid. I was grateful to receive the job offer from AIG.

I couldn't bear living in Orlando any longer, because there was a lot of drama in that house, and I was not used to that sort of chaos. Kim would open my mail, and then say she didn't see my name on the envelope! I let the married man know that I would be moving at the end of October to Sanford! I told him that I had stayed at her home for nearly three months, and that was too long. Thankfully, I had found an apartment at Stonebrook Apartments, which was closer to my job at AIG. Before I could say another word, he offered to help me move. The next day, he loaded up my belongings in our vehicles and followed me to my new place. After we got everything inside, I waited for furniture to be delivered, while he went to Publix to grab us some subs for lunch.

My apartment was on the third floor. It had vaulted ceilings, which made the place feel larger than it was. The theme I was going for was an African vibe. I had chocolate-colored furniture with a large picture of a lioness with her cub, an elephant with its baby, and a giraffe (no baby). And of course, we all know that those animals could have never been together peacefully in a real photo. I hanged that picture over the sectional, I hanged some African masks that I found at the flea market, and I had sheer cheetah-print curtains and sheer soft brown curtains, to mix the panels, so that I could deliver the feel of what I wanted. My kitchen had my favorite flowers always on the bar. I love sunflowers, and even the artificial ones gave the feel of authenticity.

My bedroom was decorated with memorabilia of my favorite football team, the Carolina Panthers. The only thing I was waiting for was my bed and the rest of my bedroom furniture. My parents came down from North Carolina with their friends, and when the furniture got there, the men carried it up to my bedroom. They struggled getting my mother up three flights of stairs, because she was seated in her wheelchair (my mother had an aneurysm and a stroke when I was 12-years-old, and she's been in a wheelchair ever since). This was the first weekend that the married man was not at my place, but he still texted me to see how everything was going. That night, he ended his text with, "I'm falling in like with you." I did not respond. I figured Halloween's full moon had impacted him somehow.

After my parents' departure, I resumed studying for my 2-20 licensing exam, which allows individuals to sell and service property, casualty, marine, surety, and health insurance in Florida. I don't why I always felt great tension when I was being tested with a time limit— perhaps it was due to having a grade-point average of less than one in high school. The next day, when I was about to respond to the married man's text, I received a call from the leasing office letting me know that they finally had a one-bedroom available on the first floor. It was what I was supposed to have initially, but considering my circumstances, I needed to get out of the house of chaos in Orlando! I told one of my coworkers, a pastor named Conrad Reid, that I needed help moving, and to my surprise, he agreed to help me move.

I gave the married man I'd been seeing a key to my apartment. He was paying my utilities and my car insurance; he made sure I had money for lunch and that I kept a full tank of gas. The only time he said I'd have to repay him was the 2-20 test fee if I did not pass. I left that building with my license in my hand! I could sell insurance in any state where AIG conducted business. As if he needed a reason to see me, the married told me that he was taking me to LongHorn Steakhouse to celebrate. He was really checking a lot of boxes, but the fact remained that he was a married man with a baby carrot.

I wanted to continue celebrating over that weekend, and I decided that I was going to go on one of the casino cruises that sailed out of Port Canaveral daily—this wasn't like the normal cruise—these ships sailed out into international water for four or five hours, before returning to dock at the port. Cruising on these ships was exclusively for gambling in the casino—think of it as a sailing casino. The married man agreed to go with me, although he had no clue where we'd end up. It was hilarious for me to see his uneasiness. It was obvious he didn't know that I knew his home address. The route to Port Canaveral took us in the direction of the city where he lived. It was funny to see him was low-key panicking. I mean, I have been messy in my past, but damn! I could have never delivered that woman's husband to her front door. I had to keep talking about funny stuff to mask the fact that I was really laughing at how uncomfortable he was. When we drove beyond the city where he lived, he let out the biggest sigh of relief, and said, "Whew! I am still full." I wanted to ask him, "Full of what?" because we hadn't gone anywhere yet to eat. I allowed him to drive my SUV to get us back to my place. I guess he felt he knew the best roads to take, to avoid any chances of seeing his wife.

As we neared my apartment, he said to me that he felt like I was avoiding the fact that he'd said he was falling in like with me, and I finally said to him, "What does that even mean?" By this time, we were back at my place, allowing the evening to unfold.

He looked me in my eyes and said, "You know the feeling you have when you're close to being in love? Well, that's what being in like means." I was in no mood for more weirdness. First, my last man had told me I'd been an experiment, now this man was "falling in like." I told him that I *had* given what he'd said some thought, and that I had written a poem as a result of him telling me that. I told him not to get all mushy, because it wasn't that type of poem, but I hoped he liked it anyway. The poem was titled "He & She" and it went like this:

> She couldn't wait to see him.
> Still, he asked for her to wait.
> She said, "I have to get there,
> Before it's far too late."
> He told her, "Just be patient,
> Our time has yet to come."
> She said, "I have to get there.
> I have to get this done."
> He said, "If you insist,
> I guess you may come by.
> You know that I am busy,
> Although we still can try."
> She said, "There's no one else,
> That will do it like you can.
> Just cancel everything.
> You know you are the man."
> He said, "I'll get you in,
> But you'll need to get here soon.

Although you'll need to be here,
Before this afternoon."
So, I'm sure you could imagine,
It's really plain to see.
The room was rather private,
For players, he and she.
"You're just in time, my dear,
Come in and close the door.
Have a seat, my darling,
Let's do what we are here for."
"I'd like to be more comfortable,
Please put my mind at ease."
He said, "It will be simple,
But here, we'll put on these."
She says, "Are you sure?
I've heard these things will bust."
He said, "I will be gentle,
Just have a LITTLE trust!"
She whispered, "Will it hurt?"
"Of course not," he replied.
"It's just a simple process,
Now lay back and open wide."
She said, "I am afraid,
I've never done this before."
He wanted to continue,
"I won't hurt you anymore."
It must be rather painful,
As tears flowed down her eyes.
She looked with much confusion,
It must be big in size.
"Please be patient darling,"
The pain untold her sin.
"Now open up much wider,

So I can get more in."
Suddenly with a jump,
She gave a little shout.
"Now it's all over darling."
And he S L O W L Y pulled it out.
Now as you will need
A dentist, I'm sure you'll find.
It's not what you were thinking,
It's just your dirty mind!

When he looked up from the paper, I asked him if he could take me to my dentist appointment the next day, because I was being sedated to have wisdom teeth extractions. He seemed perturbed by the fact that I was not addressing his "falling in like" comment. I mean, he was still married! What would I look like, allowing myself to fall deeply for him? Holidays especially reminded me that he was married, as I didn't see or hear from him then. I was growing tired of being a mistress.

I guess he was in his feelings, because he actually had the audacity to ask me why I wasn't into giving him oral sex. I was thinking, *Where did this damn question come from? Has he always wanted to ask me this shit? Wait! What the fuck did this nigga just say to me? Does he not realize that he has a baby carrot? So, in reality, what is there to actually suck?* I am sure my face said all of what I did not verbalize.

However, I was not about to come unglued, so I simply told him, "Those are wifely duties. You have a wife at home for those chores!" We were in the second year of our situationship, and I no longer felt the same way as I had for him initially. I asked him for my door key back, but he wouldn't return it, because he wasn't ready to let go of "us." I was over us and wanted to just move on with my life. Well, one day, I allowed him to use my car to go to work; plus, he wanted to make certain I had a full tank of gas. Okay. Cool. When he returned my Explorer Sport to me, he left his cell phone on the passenger's seat. Of course, I went through his phone to find his wife's phone number, and I stored her number in my phone.

This occurred around the same time that I was trying to find a surgeon back home in Charlotte to perform a breast reduction on me. The married man opposed the surgery, but he didn't have to be bothered with that weight on his neck, back, and shoulders every single day, so I continued with the plan for surgery.

I was out of work on FMLA, the Family and Medical Leave Act allows for up to 12 weeks of leave from a job for medical and other reasons, so I had enough time to spend with my parents without feeling rushed to return home. I arrived a week prior to my surgery, because some of my old party crew was going out to an all-male revue. And there was no way I was going to miss out on that. But baby! Let me tell you, a good time was definitely had that night! I'm still trying to figure out how in the hell the dancer raised both of my arms in the air, and at the same time had my damn bra in his hands, swirling it around! I needed to have some fun, because at that point, I hadn't had a girl's night out, in at least a decade.

My surgery was on April 5, 2005, and I was ready! I arrived at Presbyterian Main (today, the name is Novant Health) just as the surgeon had told me to. He reintroduced himself, the phlebotomist introduced himself, and then the doctor asked me to stand so that he could mark the areas that would be cut. The surgeon explained to me that my cup size would be a C permanently. I was elated! When I was finally released from the hospital, Mrs. Jackson, my mother's home health aide, was at the house with my mom. Mrs. Jackson worked Monday through Friday from nine o'clock in the morning until four o'clock in the afternoon. Now, some of those mornings she was late, but she never called out of work. She was faithful.

Mrs. Jackson had been a caregiver for my mother since I was 14 years old, so she was more like a second mother than an aide. It was because of Mrs. Jackson that I learned how to fry the hell out of some chicken! She taught me how to make cornbread from scratch, including Mexican-style cornbread. I even learned how to properly fold a fitted sheet because of her. She was the first person who gave a voice to what she saw in me. She told me one day, "Everything you know today, you taught yourself. You had a rough upbringing, but I am proud of who you became, because you didn't allow those things to harden you." I would make sure she received a Mother's Day gift, a birthday gift, and a Christmas gift every year, even while I lived in Florida.

I had just sat down after changing my bandages when I received a call from the married man. He said that he knew I was away having surgery and that he wanted to check on me to see how everything had gone. I told him that all was well and that I felt a noticeable difference already. He didn't really seem to be too interested in what I was saying, because he proceeded to tell me that he had stopped by my place to make sure everything looked okay.

But I was not okay with it because this joker fixed his mouth to ask me, "Can I bring someone over to your place?" The first thing that came to mind was that it was most likely a woman—and I wasn't there, so technically, he could have done whatever he wanted to do without my consent or knowledge.

"No," I told him. "Not only that, but how do I know that you haven't had someone over to my place already?"

"I would never disrespect you like that," he claimed.

I didn't believe him. I mean, hell, he had been cheating on his wife for two years at that point. I felt myself getting boiling hot! I had to calm myself down, because I didn't want my mother or Mrs. Jackson asking me what was wrong. I didn't want to lie to them, and I didn't want to admit that I had been seeing a married man. After all, they had both dealt with cheating husbands in their marriages.

I needed to return to my place in Florida to get more clothes, but due to the doctor's orders, I could not drive myself. I called my six-foot teddy bear, the man that I had shared five years of my life with. I let him know that I needed to go to Florida to get some things, and asked him if he could be my driver. Without hesitation, he showed up and drove me the entire way there.

He smoked Newport cigarettes. I asked him for a cigarette, but he knew that I had quit smoking and gave me a firm "no"! When we stopped to get gas, I watched him go inside the store to pay, and I grabbed his pack of cigarettes and took a few out.

Rogue.

I picked back up a habit that I thought I'd defeated. And you know what? If he couldn't tell that some of his cigarettes were missing, I wasn't going to open my mouth to let him know anything.

He got me back to Charlotte on time for my follow-up appointment. I am forever grateful that he remained a good friend after we split up.

During my follow-up visit with the doctor in June, he said that I could drive back home to Florida. I said my goodbyes, gave lots of hugs, said lots of prayers, and got on the road.

After I got settled in, showered, and relaxed, I called the married man. He didn't answer the phone, so I texted him, "Could you drop my key off, please?" I sent that text around one o'clock on a Tuesday afternoon. When I didn't hear from him by Thursday, I walked to the leasing office and told them that I was locked out of my apartment. I told them that I had just returned to Florida from Charlotte, and that I had lost the key to my apartment between there and here.

Without a maintenance order, someone immediately walked with me to my apartment, changed the lock, and gave me a new set of keys. Since the married man didn't want to return my key and had ignored my text, I felt it was time to turn up the heat! His wife's home phone and cell phone numbers had been stored in my phone for over a year. I decided to call whichever one my finger landed on first, and she answered the phone.

"Hello?" she said cheerfully. This was not a social call, and I was tired of repeating myself. Her husband didn't want to accept the fact that I no longer wanted to see him, and he wouldn't return my door key. So I simply said, "Your husband is cheating on you."

Her cheery voice turned into rage, and rightfully so. "Who is this?"

she exclaimed.

"His mistress, of course," I said. I don't know if the call dropped or if she actually hung up the phone, but I was done being a secret. I didn't want him in my life any longer. I really felt awful for my part in the affair, but he didn't want to let go of "us" and he would not accept that there was no us.

That evening, the married man called. I answered and immediately I heard the brokenness in his voice.

"Aye! Yo," he said. "That was foul, yo. How could you do that to—" Before he could even complete his sentence, his wife got on the line and started bombarding me with questions. I had nothing to hide, and I certainly did not owe her an explanation. I didn't have loyalty to her; that was his duty. When she asked me how long we had been seeing each other, he told her not to worry about all of that. I was not about to exchange words with this woman about a damn baby carrot!

I allowed her to speak her piece, and after she was done, I said to her, "As I woman, I can admit that I was wrong for being involved with a married man. Every time I tried to break things off with him, he would show up with a gift of some kind and smooth things over. I was not happy being the other woman. I was wrong for being the other woman, and I apologize that it happened to you."

"I expect you not to see him again!" she told me. I had been cordial up until that point when she felt like barking orders at me.

"For the record, you can also expect there to be stormy weather in Florida," I said to her. "If he calls me and tells me he wants to see me, best believe my door will always be open! If you'd like to discuss this in person, your husband knows my address!" I hung up the phone and turned it off for the rest of the night. I also took the house phone off the hook, because the married man knew that number, too.

About two months after returning to work, I was still ignoring text messages and phone calls from the married man. On a day when I decided to work overtime, I spoke on the phone with a man in California whose voice was a cross between Barry White's and James Earl

Jones's. He had my full attention! On top of that, he spoke like an educated man, and that was impressive to me. I already knew that he had immaculate credit, because AIG did not advertise to people with less-than-perfect credit scores. But I remained professional and handled the call appropriately.

I completed my shift, and on my way out, I noticed a travel agency's flyer for a weekend cruise to the Bahamas. Just out of curiosity, I called the number, to see if what was on the flyer was accurate, and the woman who answered the phone confirmed everything that I had read.

When I got home, I called my sister Tonya, and my cousin Sondra to see if either of them would be interested in going on the cruise with me. Even though my sister and I had times in our relationship when we didn't always see eye to eye, I mean, doesn't that happen between sisters? You forgive, well, at least I forgave her, and moved on. I didn't hold a grudge… forgiveness is not about letting a person off the hook for any wrongs they've done to others. I was ready to put *man trouble* behind me and enjoy myself on a cruise. Neither of them needed to be convinced to go on the cruise. They sent their money, and we paid for our trip swiftly.

My sister was not a licensed driver at the time, so my cousin drove down to Florida from Charlotte, and we went in my car to Port Canaveral where the cruise ships were docked. I managed to get on board with some ganja, and I shared with my cousin because my sister did not smoke ganja. When my sister saw the joint in my hand, she sat up on her bed and pointed her finger at me, with her other hand on her hip as if to scold me.

"You got durn devil!" she said to me. "Now, Imma tell mama! How did you get that on this ship, Angie?" I looked at my cousin, and we burst into uncontrollable laughter. When I think back on how I got it on the ship, I realize I could have actually gone to jail! I had micro-braids in my hair. I rolled the ganja and placed it inside of the cellophane wrapper from a cigarette pack. Next, I placed the wrapper on the center of my scalp and made a small ponytail around it. Then I pulled the rest of the microbraids up over the ponytail and made a lazy bun. Undetected.

I got high as a damn kite on that cruise. Our first cruise, but not our last cruise. We had so much fun! Oh, my goodness, I think we slept maybe 20 hours that whole weekend.

We did not want to get off of that ship! Royal Caribbean owed us nothing! When we finally did get off and left the port, I think I missed our exit three different times while driving home. Two of those times, we were going in the same direction. Thank God, we finally made it back to my apartment, because I was sleepy and felt like I was still on the ship, moving.

My sister and cousin had to get on the road, so they could get home to Charlotte. My sister left without telling me that she had purposely filled my toilet with that thick-ass Charmin tissue to clog it. That evening was not the time to be doing pranks, because the leasing office was closed until the next day, and a clogged toilet was not considered an after-hours emergency.

When I got to work the next day, I had several voicemail messages from the Barry White/James Earl Jones–sounding man. He told me in one of the messages that he would call my line every day until I returned his call. I completed some other tasks before calling him, because I wanted to get at least 10 sales completed before I went to lunch. I was not a real salesperson, and I honestly hated that job. Some of my coworkers could sell fire to the gates of hell, but I was not in that league.

Randy Price, in my opinion, was one of the best salespeople in the building, he was consistent in meeting his sales goals. He was someone I could confide in without feeling like I was being judged, which is one of the reasons why he became one of my dearest friends.

I eventually got promoted to the claims department, which I was proud of, but being on that team made me realize that while I was in corporate, it still was not my ideal job. I didn't like talking on the phones to people who thought I was saying my name was Nancy! It was mostly elderly ladies that called me Nancy, and I just went with it. I was exhausted trying to get them to understand that I had said, "Angie. Not Nancy." My teammates started teasing me and calling me Nancy. I went along with the jokes, because it was actually funny.

One day, two calls decided my fate with AIG. The first call was a mother reporting that her daughter had been killed in an auto accident. I was not prepared for that. I didn't know how to shut off my emotions, and I silently cried with that mother. Thankfully, the team leader was nearby, because she had been monitoring that particular call, and she told me to go on break, that she would complete the call for me. I did as she suggested, and I must have walked around the entire building at least three or four times. When it felt like my head was clear enough to take the next call, sadly, it was also a death call. I told the team leader that I would be taking the rest of the day off, and that I wouldn't be in the next day either.

During those days out of office, I went online and applied to some companies who were hiring human resource assistants. I heard back rather quickly from a construction company and accepted their job offer. Thankfully, I had not quit AIG yet, because the new job wouldn't begin for around two weeks. The pay for the HR assistant job was significantly more than what AIG had been paying me, but the commute was a nightmare! I lived in Sanford, and had to drive to Winter Park— about a 40-minute drive without traffic. I hated driving on I-4, so I would always take 17/92, and get caught at every redlight.

# The Man From California

In 2005, the Barry White/James Earl Jones–sounding California man and I had been talking on the phone and sending morning texts to one another for about eight months. We were eager to finally meet one another in person. I had sent him several pictures of myself. Meanwhile, he kept saying that he didn't like taking pictures. He told me that a lot of people had told him that he looked a lot like Avery Brooks... you know, the brother whose character's name was Hawk on the '80s TV show called *Spenser for Hire*. He would tell me how gorgeous I was. I knew I wasn't as beautiful as Janet Jackson or Missy Elliott, who are both gorgeous, in my opinion. I had my bullshit detector on, and I said to myself, "Self!" Self said, "Huh?" Then, summarized that this dude was hiding his face for a reason.

After I asked him a third time if he had remembered to take a selfie, I realized that he had to have a face that told stories—maybe too many.

He already had introduced me to his oldest sister via three-way call. Her name was Kimberley, but everyone called her Kim. From the first time we spoke on the phone, our friendship took off like a bolt of lightning. I liked the fact that she was so transparent and withheld no details about her brother. She let me know that he had a bit of a control issue, but my personality would be able to contain him.

She also told me that he had said to her that he wanted to marry me. I was shocked, to say the least. I mean, here it was eight months since we had been talking on the phone and through text messages, and he'd never said, "Let's get married!"

I told her flat out, "I am not ready for all of that!" It was like my spirit answered before my brain could filter my response. I don't know if what I said registered, because she went on to tell me about her children and how they loved their uncle. She also mentioned that her brother wanted a child. This time I stayed quiet, because I knew damn well that I wasn't about to be trying to push a whole human out of me!

Then the day came when he wanted me to meet his mother, Miss Penny, over the phone. Honey, Miss Penny hated the air that I breathed. Why? Because her son, with his grown ass, had decided he was going to move from California to Florida to start a life with me. I had never gotten any objections from anyone's parent. Especially not a mother. But she already had hatred toward me before I'd even met her.

Initially, I had spoken with him about coming to Florida for a visit. He already knew that I was going home to Charlotte for Christmas, and he agreed to help me drive up there. I thought he would just be taking vacation time for our visit. When his oldest sister, Kim, learned how rude and nasty their mother had been toward me, she spoke up on my behalf. Then, here comes his younger sister on the phone with her two cents. She sided with her mama, even though she didn't know me from a can of paint. I knew that I did not want to marry into dysfunction, especially since I had grown up with abnormalities in my own family.

Kim told me that her brother wanted me to think he was coming solely for a visit, but he'd already arranged for a moving company to transport his vehicles and a different company to haul his clothing from California to Florida.

The day that I picked him up from the airport, I wanted to leave without him! I saw in person, with my own two eyes, the reason he had not wanted to send a selfie. I thought to myself, *Oh my God! His face! How in the hell does a voice that sounds like Barry White and James Earl Jones belong to that face?*

His mother's genes were so strong! Absolutely nothing about him resembled his father.

Good Lord!

I remember him telling me that his mother was a twin, and before

I knew it, I said, "I hope she's not an identical twin." He took that to mean that his mother's demeanor had embarrassed him. Side eye. I knew that it meant I had met a dude who looked like he was really from the *Planet of the Apes.*

After we left the airport, he wanted to stop and get lunch before we went back to my place. And honestly, I did not want to be seen in public with him. He wanted authentic Mexican food, and I told him we could go down 436 and we'd probably find something. Good thing I followed my gut instinct, because not even two miles down 436, we came to a restaurant called Ponchos. I could smell the grilled onions and peppers before we even got in the door. He ordered a stuffed shrimp burrito, and I got the lunch special—nachos with a smaller burrito.

I offered him some of my food, and he said his burrito would be enough, yet somehow, his hands kept removing nachos from my plate. Okay. I was sick of that immediately! I slid the plate of nachos to him without saying a word, because I'd offered it to him, he'd declined, and then he'd proceeded to stick his hands in my plate. He said, "I don't want anymore." I told him I didn't either, because I was full. I wasn't full, but his hands had been in my plate more than my own!

I had heard of "fake it until you make it," but I didn't know how to fake a relationship with him.

In the weeks that followed, I learned that he had OCD so bad that it drove me nuts!

I was sick of him from the first day that he came to Florida. Prior to moving to Florida, we had spoken on the phone in great length about my road-trip home for Christmas to visit with my family. He let me know that his flight would be landing the week prior to Christmas Day, so that gave him a few days to familiarize himself with his new surroundings. Funny how he never exposed how controlling he was; I learned that once he stepped foot across the threshold of my apartment.

The time had come for us to take our road-trip to Charlotte, but I was not looking forward to an eight-hour drive to Charlotte and another eight hours back with him.

He met my parents, and about 30 minutes into our visit, my mom said she had to use the bathroom. Being that she needed assistance, I pushed her in her wheelchair to the bathroom, and I turned the water on full blast so that it could drown out our whispers.

"Ma! There is no way that I can be with that man," I told her.

In a loving yet curious voice, she said, "Why?"

"Did you see his damn face?" I said.

My mother was laughing so hard, she could barely get herself together. She looked at me and tried not to laugh. Then she said, "Well, is he good in bed?" I paused. Considering there had been a baby carrot in my life prior to this man from California, it was not a major improvement, and he definitely was not mind-blowing.

I tried to remain cordial with him, but I felt like I had been bamboozled.

I knew I did not want to be with the man from California.

Omission is still a lie, right? We could have saved his mother the unnecessary attitude she had toward me, if only he had sent a picture of his whole face when I had asked for one repeatedly. The moment I'd lost interest and quit asking him for a picture, he finally sent one. But it showed only the side of his damn face. Then he sent a picture where his ball cap covered his eyes, and the shadow from the bib of the cap covered his nose. When I tell you that he put the "orang" in "orangutan," I am not exaggerating!

On our drive back to Florida, I was so annoyed with him that I suggested we move into a two-bedroom apartment instead of staying together in my one-bedroom. Before he could ask why, I told him that I knew he had a lot of clothes, and my closet was not going to be able to hold all of my things and his. I sold him on having his own walk-in closet in the second bedroom. He liked the idea, and said that the second room could be his man cave. I didn't add to anything he said. I agreed with him, because it meant I didn't have to see his face when I awakened every morning.

I am by no means shallow, but damn. That face!

We moved into Sail Pointe Apartments, directly across the street from Lake Monroe—still in Sanford, but we were now in the downtown area. That town was so small, it reminded me of Mayberry, that fictional town in *The Andy Griffith Show*.

Then in May 2006, two bad things happened: my Ford Explorer Sport got repossessed, and in the same week, my cousin Vern called and told me that Mr. Panama Man had died of a heart attack. The repossession occurred due to me paying all of the bills and rent by myself. I was receiving little to no help from the man from California; so, my car payments got further and further behind.

The man from California had a strong desire to control me, particularly where I went in his car. He told me that I was allowed to go only to and from work and to the gas station to refill his tank. I was not to go to any other places without his permission. I know I had an "excuse me, motherfucker" look on my face. I walked up to him and looked him in his cockeyes and said, "Understand me when I tell you this: I am 33-plus, a damn woman! The last time I checked, your name was not on my damn birth certificate. You've got me fucked up with your exes that you had control of. I'm a whole lot of woman, so even on your best day, you do not put fear in me. I grew up getting my ass beat, and I'll be damned if I let a motherfucker put his goddamn hands on me!"

All he could say was, "Angela, nobody said they were going to touch you. But that's my damn car, and if you don't like my rules, you can just get to where you need to go the best way you can! You ain't gone talk no shit to me and need me, too!"

Given my history, I told myself not to do anything crazy, because my win was coming, and I would not allow the "when" to worry me.

The very next day, I took his car without his permission. He saw me grab the keys and head toward the door.

I mean, what was he going to do?

I wasn't about to tell him where I was going, because if he wanted to know badly enough, he would've gotten in his other car and followed me.

I went to Altamonte Springs to see a broker, and I sold the shares of stock that I had purchased while I was employed with the insurance company, AIG. When I got back to the apartment, I got on my computer, changed the password, and searched for a car on DriveTime's website. Selling the stock shares gave me enough money for a down payment, along with two additional car payments, so that I was already ahead. When I was ready to go pick up my car, I told the man from California that I needed a ride to DriveTime. I knew which one I needed to go to, but because he wanted to be an ass, he took me to a different one and left! I went inside the building and spoke with some representatives to inform them of what had happened. They were kind enough to call their other store, and the salesperson that I had been communicating with online came to that location to pick me up. By the end of the night, I had keys to my own ride!

The year seemed to be moving at a rapid pace.

I spoke with my sister and updated her about how ugly the man from California was, inside and out.

His sister had not lied when she said he was controlling, and I hadn't lied when I told her he'd catch hell trying to control me.

We had a cruise planned in October for his birthday, but I was not looking forward to going.

The day of our departure, the drive to Cape Canaveral was long and daunting. I didn't say anything the whole way, until I saw vultures perched on the supertall light posts. I literally said, "Oooooh! Heckle and Jeckle!" I had never seen a vulture in real life. The closest creatures were the cartoon characters Heckle and Jeckle, although they were magpies. He tried to look up and drive at the same time and ended up crossing into the oncoming traffic's lane; I was determined not to talk to him, so I said nothing. Thankfully, no other cars were on the road!

We made it to the port safely, paid for parking, and boarded the ship.

When the ship got to the Bahamas, I awakened him and told him that we had docked, and asked him if he wanted to get off the ship. Well, he assed around until he missed the opportunity to go tour the island! Then he had the audacity to blame me for his missing the opportunity. He stormed off and went in one direction, and I went in the other. I did not want to be seen with him anyway!

I went to the ship's concierge desk to check my bank balance, and found out that he had been using my money to pay for what he wanted on the ship, instead of using his own! I told the concierge clerk that I was the only person to use my card and no one else! After that fiasco, I went back to the cabin to shower and prepare for dinner. I was applying my Midnight Pomegranate lotion by Bath & Body Works when the cabin door opened.

He looked furious!

In a raised voice, he said to me, "Why the hell would you allow me to get embarrassed? When I tried to use the cabin card to pay for my stuff, they told me I couldn't use it—or 'declined,' or whichever they said."

"Embarrassed?" I said. "How's that my problem? Did you add funds to your cabin keycard?"

He rolled his eyes so hard and let the door slam behind him as he left.

I told myself, *There has to be a way to get out of this shit.* Because no way in hell I was I going to keep putting up with a manipulative control freak with a severe case of OCD!

Thanksgiving came and went, and during that holiday weekend, I spoke with my sister Tonya by phone, and she said she'd be coming to Florida with our parents and our great-auntie Sarah.

I was happy to see my family. My parents and auntie checked into a hotel that was lakefront, and my sister stayed at my apartment with me and the man from California. She thought I had been lying about how the man from California looked. She also thought I was being overly sensitive about him. Then, during her visit, she heard him trying to talk shit to me! He thought everyone was gone, but my sister was in the bathroom inside of my bedroom.

My sister gave him hell!

"Meet my black ass outside, because I don't want to tear up any of my sister's shit," she told him. "And I'll be damned if you gone talk to my motherfucking sister like that!" I was relieved that she saw that I had not been lying about him.

***

One morning in January of the following year, I saw a U-Haul truck parked outside near my SUV. I didn't think much of it, and got in my car and went to work. When I returned to the apartment, everything except my furniture was gone, and the man from California was gone, too. He'd taken a lot of my things, and that was okay. I was glad to have his monkey ass out of my life!

I called the leasing office to transfer to a one-bedroom apartment. I told the woman that I no longer needed a two-bedroom, and she accommodated my request.

The man from California thought he had broken me, but he didn't know that I am resilient. My bounce-back is quick. While I may curse some and I enjoy my ganja, I still know who God is.

I also know that without faith, it is impossible to please God.

I sat down and reflected on what I had endured while I was with him. Initially I told myself that I had gone through all that because I'd been with another woman's husband.

Karma?

Perhaps.

In reality, I went through a lot of what I did because I allowed shit to happen. That man thought I needed him, but the truth was, he needed me.

He didn't know that I knew his new address. *Well, duh! You used my damn computer!* I went to Walgreens and bought a 99-cent greeting card and mailed it to his address, to congratulate him on his new home. It wasn't even a real gift. I was just letting him know that I knew where he lived.

He must've been pissed off that I knew his new home address, because he clipped me in the worse way! He and I were on the same plan with Cingular Wireless. Technically, it was his cellular plan, meaning he owned my phone number. And he abruptly shut off my line.

I called the wireless provider to see if I could reactivate the number by establishing my own account, and they told me no. I asked why not.

"The phone number was on a plan that belongs to a different individual," the representative told me. "That means they own the number, so you would have to get permission from the account owner to have ownership of the phone number."

It was especially bad not to have access to my phone number, because I was waiting on a follow-up call from a company I'd recently interviewed with. They were going to call to let me know my start date and details about orientation.

The man from California was so determined to control me that he'd allow such an important opportunity to pass.

I got my own line and didn't give him my number.

One day, out of the blue, he popped up at my place to check on me. I didn't think I needed to put my new phone away before allowing him into my place, because it was my place!

He discovered my phone while I'd excused myself to the bathroom. He called himself from my phone, so that he'd have my number. Then he deleted his number from my call log so that his number wasn't the last one dialed from my phone.

Controlling.

Possessive.

At some point, he got off his high horse and wanted to be cordial again. I told him that that part of our lives was a closed chapter. I could not see myself ever having romantic feelings for him again. He pleaded with me to come to his home to see how he had decorated, and like a fool, I went, even knowing it was going to be some bullshit. We made small talk. It was near Memorial Day, and according to him, he had fireworks that he had been shooting off. He asked me if I could teach him to make coleslaw the same way that I always made mine, and I told him no because it was a family recipe. His home wasn't in the best neighborhood, but it was nice. The exterior was like a soft blueish mint color that covered the stucco. Inside, he had basically copied my living room style, the only difference is his furniture was faux leather. He had a three-bedroom, one bath, and the laundry room was inside a space at the back of the kitchen—it actually led to his back door. The floor plan reminded me a lot of the duplex I lived in, in Creektown. Once I had seen what I went to see, I was prepared to leave and go back to my place.

Before I left, I was seated at his kitchen table while he finished up his phone call with the California DMV. I was about to leave, until I heard him say something about a DUI on his record. I was perplexed, because he'd told me that he quit drinking in 2003, and here it was 2007, and I'm hearing him talking to California's DMV about a DUI charge that occurred in 2005, before he moved to Florida!

What?

This dude was an undercover alcoholic!

How in the hell had I missed that?

He was an expert at being deceitful and manipulative! Visiting hours were over for me, and I went out his door. The next thing I knew, he threw a firecracker at my feet, and I jumped in the air! He *literally* scared the piss out of me! I walked toward him to punch him, but he ran in his house and locked the door. I showered when I got home, because, well… I peed my pants.

Something about the firecracker being thrown at my feet unlocked a repressed memory that I didn't ask for.

That night, back in my own place, I awakened from a dream crying.

I called the man from California, and immediately he panicked.

"What's wrong? Did something happen?" he asked. "Angela! Speak to me! What is wrong?"

I was crying so hard and still trying to catch my breath to tell him what I had just experienced.

"Did I ever tell you about the time when the crime lab came to our house when I was 12 years old?" I managed to ask him.

Sounding puzzled, he assured me that I had never mentioned anything to him about it.

"It's a long story," I said.

"It's fine. I want to help you through whatever you're going through," he said.

I blew my nose, wiped away the tears pouring from my eyes, and told him, "My mom had come home from the physical therapy rehabilitation part of the hospital. She had had an aneurysm and later had a stroke that paralyzed the left side of her body. My father brought her home, and he left, because he wasn't actually living with us at the time, and he was an absent father. He had gone to Family Dollar and bought my mom a cheap jacket, and since I didn't have one to wear to school, I asked her if I could wear hers. She told me yes. When he came to the house to pick her up, he asked her where her jacket was, and she told him that I'd worn it to school. She allowed him to believe that I had taken it without her permission; perhaps she was afraid of what he'd do. After all, aside from being domestic violence occurring in our household, my father was often unfaithful to my mother. I mean, come on now, we're talking about a no-name-brand wannabe Members Only jacket. My auntie, my mother's sister, said that she told my mom she ought not lie on me, because she did tell me that I could wear her jacket to school." He listened while I told him about what had happened to me.

He sounded like he'd sniffled a little, but I proceeded to tell him, "When I stepped off the school bus, my brother met me at my stop, which was odd, because he never did that. He told me, 'Daddy is looking for you, because he said he's going to whip you.' I asked him for what, because I hadn't done anything wrong. I was afraid to go home, so I went to the home of one of my friends. My brother knew where I was and came back again, this time to actually get me. When I walked in the door, I immediately heard my absent father yelling at me to go upstairs to their bedroom and take off my clothes. I stripped down butt naked, and he beat me like a runaway slave with no papers! He beat me to the point that the skin on my butt had been split open to the fleshy white meat. The cuts on my skin came from the switches—more like small branches—that he used."

Tears streamed from my eyes. This time, I was certain that I could hear the shock in his subtle reaction. He was actually crying. He was living my experience with me as I told him, "My auntie called the police, the crime lab came out, and they took lots of pictures. My father was afraid of the police, which meant he wasn't going to come back to our house to get my mom anytime soon. He would call and want to talk to me on the phone, but he never apologized. He made empty promises, trying to get me to agree to move with him and my mom to a duplex. In that moment, I knew that I strongly disliked him. I know the Bible tells us that if we hate, then in our hearts we've already committed murder. If that were the case, then why isn't he dead?"

The man from California had definitely started crying at some point. I don't even know when that was. He apologized to me for my having to endure something like that as a child. He also apologized for throwing the firecracker at my feet, which possibly triggered that repressed memory.

That is the one time that I can say for sure that the man from California was a true friend. He offered to take me to dinner and a movie. He didn't say when, though.

That man was so frugal! He waited until *Why Did I Get Married?* was showing at the Colonial 8 Cinemas, where the cover charge was only a dollar. Before I left my place, I figured that since he was cutting costs, I'd better take my oversized purse and put some cold bottles of water in it, along with some theater candy. While he was cheap, the movie theater thankfully was in a nice area. We were in the shopping plaza where there was a Kmart, a Hallmark store, a pub called the Blue

Whale, and an Albertson's grocery store.

After the movie, we went to a Chinese buffet for dinner. He was so full, he laid down on the seat in our booth. Other customers were looking.

I took his wallet from his pocket, paid for our food with one of his cards, and went to my car.

*You are not about to embarrass me any longer!*

I called his phone when I got to my car and asked him how long he planned to sleep in those folks' restaurant.

Not long after the movie and dinner, he was pissy drunk! He drove himself to my apartment, but I wouldn't let him in until he said he'd just hit a motorcycle. Being that he lived within two miles of where the incident occurred (the incident was in the parking lot of my apartment complex), he decided he'd leave the scene of the accident and walk home. But he'd left his keys in his car, so that meant he had locked himself out of his house. I was not about to help him mask a crime, and wanted nothing to do with it. But really, I refused to help him because he had given one of his exes my phone number and told her to call me and ask me to call a locksmith. He got so angry when I refused to call a locksmith to go grant him access to his house.

I cursed his ex 30 ways from Sunday. She was defensive and said she was only doing what he'd told her to do, and that she couldn't understand why I was upset.

"If he told you to jump off a bridge, I guess you'll ask him which bridge!" I told her.

All of a sudden, my television quit playing. I called Brighthouse Networks to see if there was an outage in the area, and when they confirmed there wasn't one, they sent a technician out. The tech checked to make sure everything was properly connected inside my apartment, and then went outside to check for any issues.

When the young man returned to my door, he said, "Ma'am, someone disconnected the cable line outside, which is why you're not receiving service."

He reset the cable box, and my TV started playing again.

A little while later, the man from California called and asked, "What are you watching on TV?" He was laughing like he'd told the best joke. It was obvious in that moment that he was the one who'd disconnected my cable, all because I had not felt the obligation to call a locksmith.

"I'm in my apartment out of the rain. Why don't you call the police and tell them what you did? Tell them that you hit my neighbor's motorcycle and left the scene of an accident."

He was livid!

He hung up the phone, and I didn't hear from him again until later the next day, when he walked back to my apartment to get his car. I wasn't going to let him into my place, but he said he had to urinate really bad and there were some kids outside, and he didn't want to get arrested for public urination.

I let him in.

He used the bathroom, went to my sofa, sat down, and got comfortable.

I told him he had to leave.

Then he started with his half-assed apology, and midsentence, he fell asleep. I grabbed my mood lipstick—it was actually a shade of green, but once applied, it turned red. Since he wouldn't leave, I waited until he was snoring like a freight train, then I applied the lipstick.

It was a pretty, glossy red.

I had plans to begin classes in the fall of 2007, and he was determined he'd be a distraction. I kindly left him in the living room and went to complete my college application, and when he finally awakened, he used the bathroom again, washed his hands, and left.

I didn't open my mouth. Didn't say a word.

Maybe 44 seconds after he left, I heard a knock at my door.

I could hear him laughing as I got closer, and when I opened the door he said, "You little niglette!"

I asked, "What? What happened?"

He said, "I was driving out of the parking lot, and my cigarette slipped from between my lips. I looked in the mirror and yelled, 'ANGELA! GODDURN IT!'"

I laughed so hard and asked him, "How did you not know you had lipstick on? You used the bathroom before you left."

"I wasn't looking in the mirror," he said. "I was trying to make sure I didn't get piss on your toilet or the floor, because I didn't want to hear your dang mouth." We laughed about the moment before he left to return home.

It's sad about him, though. He was an alcoholic, he lost his role as a supervisor at a Sears warehouse, he crashed one of his cars and lost possession of the other one, and then he became homeless because he lost his house. But by the time he lost his house and his second car, his issues were no longer my concern. I changed my number and never heard from him again.

# Tenacious

I reflected back to 2002 when a former supervisor of mine made it seem as though I was a disgruntled employee with deep emotional issues. That heffa referred me to a mandatory employee assistance program. I was escorted to the appointment, and the counselor told me that she knew the supervisor was the one that needed to be in her presence, not me. She also told me that I was tenacious.

"Do you know what that word means?" she asked.

I was almost embarrassed to admit that I didn't, but what good would it have done for me to lie? I told her that I didn't know.

"Well, that's okay," she said. "You are a woman who is determined to achieve goals in life. Mediocre doesn't satisfy you. You want something greater, and I know that you will have that one day. That is what tenacious is. You are tenacious because I heard you say that you want to graduate from college. You will. I believe in you."

I lit up like a Christmas tree. I cannot recall a time when I'd ever had that much positivity spoken to me, and this had come from a complete stranger.

The counselor was right. I was determined to be something greater than I was in that moment. After leaving the man from California, I did a lot of praying before I enrolled in classes at Florida Metropolitan University (the name was later changed to Everest University). I prayed for the Lord to give me the focus I needed to be a successful student and graduate with my degree. It never occurred to me that I would be the first person from the household I'd grown up in to go to college, or even the first member from my mother's side of the family to attend college. But I was ready to be a trailblazer.

I was excited, because I realized that I was about to fulfill my desire of getting a college education. When I spoke with the enrollment counselor, I was very candid and transparent. I let him know that my high school grades were horrible.

"You know what, Angela? That is perfectly fine," he told me. "We have tutors who will assist you with any of your classes, and that is not an extra charge. We want you to be successful." Initially, I enrolled in the business management program to get an associate's degree. Then, after the term began, I had a change of heart and requested to be switched to the bachelor's degree business management program. The student services counselor tried her best to convince me to remain in the associate's program.

"Why" I asked her.

"Most students who make that decision end up dropping out of school altogether," she told me.

I took what she said as a challenge, because who TF did she think I was? I didn't come to quit this time. I came to shake and move! It was time to make some things happen!

I was excited because my classes were set to begin in the fall. Then Kim (the one who lived in Orlando and was my alleged sister) called and asked if I wanted to go to the Hard Rock casino in Tampa. I told her about my enrollment, and she said it was time to celebrate! I took $40 with me, because I was not about to give a casino all of my hard-earned money. I found a slot machine called Pharaoh's Fortune and stayed on that game the entire time we were at the casino. I kept hitting the bonus and playing the *points* back—somehow, I thought the *credits* I saw on the screen were points and not actual money. I wasn't a gambler, so I was green. When I finally cashed out, I had won back my $40 plus $200 more! That was a decent payout.

While we were driving back to Orlando to Kim's house, she asked me if I wanted to go with her to church the following week. I looked at her and jokingly said, "What's up with you holy rollers in Orlando?" She had asthma, and I felt bad that what I said made her start laughing and coughing at the same time.

"What the hell does that mean?" she asked me.

"Last week, I went to the Seminole Center, and there was a lady there who asked me if I was an evangelist," I told her. We both erupted into laughter, and then I continued: "She said to me, 'Look at your hands. You've got so much God in you that you don't know what to do with it! And I'll tell you something else, God has a story for you to tell. I hope I'm still living so that I can read the book.'"

"That sounds like 'The Prophetess,'" Kim said. I couldn't recall the lady's name, but I described her to Kim.

"That's exactly who that is," Kim said. "She is not lying to you. That woman is a real prophet." That scared me, and I hesitated to answer her question about going to church, but I went ahead and told her that I'd go. I asked her what time service began, and when she said seven o'clock at night, I asked her, "What kind of church do you go to?" She laughed and told me that her church held Bible study on Friday nights. So, on August 17, 2007, I went with Kim to her church.

Although it was a Friday night, the church was filled like it was a Sunday-morning service. I believe their church could hold 300 people with room to spare; it wasn't a huge mega church, but it wasn't small either. Kim and I sat maybe four or five rows back from the first row. Suddenly, I heard footsteps coming in our direction, and I could see in my peripheral vision people moving to the left and right. The footsteps seemed to stop right in front of me, but I was not about to look up. Nope! In my mind, I was screaming, *Gone somewhere, Mr. Head Sir Person. Whoever you are!*

I started turning the pages in my Bible like I was actually reading. I heard a voice as heavy as T. D. Jakes's say, "Excuse me, sister." Well, there were a lot of women in the church, so maybe he was not talking to me.

Mannnnn! Listen! When Kim turned like she was about to get up and sprint out of the church, my heart starting pounding. It was the bishop!

"Excuse me sister," I looked up. My eyes met his.

"You've been praying and asking God what it is that He wants you to do for Him," he told me.

I didn't let him finish. "You know, it's funny you would say that, because a prophetess—"

"I don't need to hear nothing no one else has told you." He said, interrupting me right back. Ha! "I stand before you as a man, but God is using me to tell you this. Come with me."

When I stood up, my heart was racing, my bladder became so weak, and my legs were shaking like I was about to be baptized without my knowledge or consent! I got to the altar, and I said to myself, *Ain't no way in the world this man is about to tell me that the Lord wants me to preach to anyone.*

I did not like being the center of attention. The entire church looked at me as he said, "Your pain started about 12 years ago." I looked perplexed and only shifted my eyes around the room, and did the math quickly. Sure enough, 12 years earlier, my grandfather had passed away.

"Why do you look confused?" the bishop asked me.

"Because my grandfather passed away 12 years ago," I said. Immediately, it felt like someone had knocked the breath out of me. I heard him tell someone to get me a chair, and they sat me down.

"As I stated," he continued, "I stand before you as a man, but God is using me to tell you that you have been in constant prayer, asking Him what you are supposed to do with your life. God said, 'There are some women and little girls that needs to hear from you. They can hear the same message a thousand times, but they won't understand it until it comes from your voice.' I don't know where God is going to send you, or where He is going to use you, but you do have an assignment."

I must've blacked out or something, because I do not remember anything else about that service, except for when it was over. I had never in all my 35 years of living experienced anything like that. When Kim and I were leaving, I was trying to get out of the church before the bishop could say another word to me. I waited at the back of the church near the exit for Kim to finish speaking with her fellow parishioners.

When she got closer to me, I told her, "Kim, I don't appreciate you telling your pastor about my life."

"I ain't tell him nothing!" she said, all defensive.

Then, out of nowhere, this little elderly lady who was maybe four foot five and 90 pounds soaking wet appeared and said to me, "Baby, ain't nobody gots to tell him nothing. God uses him like that."

I didn't say a word to Miss Grandma Ma'am Lady; I turned and walked out of the church as quickly as my legs could carry me. I was so discombobulated that I didn't even remember where we had parked.

That night, I dreamed that I was sitting on the toilet, and something kept trying to lift me and carry me out of the bathroom. I held on to the doorframe until my fingers were nearly blistered. I don't know if it was a ghost, as in the Holy Ghost, or if it was Jesus Himself. But I was certain that I was not going to go back to sleep that night! I stayed awake, sat on my porch, and watched the sunrise. After that experience, I did not go back to church for 104 Sundays!

The church experience from the night of August 17th took my mind back to when I was 19 years old. I had caught the city bus to my parents' home, to go with them to church one Sunday. At some point in the service, the pastor did an altar call, except I wasn't there for what he and others thought I was there for; I was there to tell him about a dream that I'd had. Being that he told me to never repeat the dream, I won't divulge what happened, but he did tell me to read Psalm 91 every night before bed. To this very day, I still recite Psalm 91 as a part of my bedtime prayer because it is a passage about protection, refuge, and God's covering.

# Humble Beginnings

I realized that I was in the season of my life where it did not have a blueprint. My life did not have a guide, and it definitely did not have a safety net. I understood that my decision to reenter college meant that I again would be the first one from my household to attend. It also meant that I was stepping onto a path that no one from my mother's side of the family had ever journeyed.

The fall term began, and I was doing my classes online. I didn't know what to expect, but I liked the whole concept of online classes because it meant that I didn't have to compete against someone else's grades. I was my own competition. One day after I submitted my first research paper, I decided to go into a Yahoo Spades game room on the web. One of the players who was not a person of color had struck up a chat with all of the players in the room. We talked about college, and what everyone was studying. When I said that I was in school for business management, his immediate response was, "Why does ALL Black people go to college for business?" Racist much? Yes! Rude? Absolutely! Other players who were also not people of color spoke up and chastised him.

After that game, I called my auntie Geneva and told her how things were going in school, but I also told her what that "pale boy," as she called him, had said to me.

"The next time you sit at a gaming table with him, tell him that you're studying psychology," she advised me.

"Aunt Gent! I don't study psychology," I told her.

"Well, you should," she said. "I think you would be good at it."

That is where my humble seed of studying psychology took root.

I heeded my auntie's advice and searched for other online colleges. When I learned that most of my credits could be transferred to Liberty University, I jumped at the opportunity. But I didn't know that Everest University had some unsavory things happening within its corridors, and I learned that the only way I could transfer those credits was if I paid backdated tuition fees. I was baffled! How was I in school all that time with a semester unpaid? I knew I didn't have the money to pay for the college transfer, so I called my mother in tears. I mean, I was crying like someone had stolen my pink bicycle with the tassels. I told her what had happened.

"Now, I want you to be a big girl for Mama," she told me. "Stop crying. I will send you the money." By the following week, Everest University had been paid, the majority of my credits had transferred, and I was officially a student at Liberty University, all thanks to my mama! After getting that situation squared away, in 2010 I moved back to my parents' home in Charlotte, NC, just in time for football season. I loved my Carolina Panthers. I went from broken Point A, which was having a GPA that was less than one in high school, to polished Point B, graduating with a 3.38 GPA for my bachelor's of science in psychology degree! But you know what? The real victory wasn't the GPA—it was what that degree taught me about myself. That psychology degree helped me to recognize my brokenness. It taught how to forgive past hurts. Those studies made me reflect on how much I needed to change, and to apologize to some folks that I had offended. Those folks didn't have to forgive me for anything; they didn't owe me that. I needed to own the wrongs that I'd done and the hurts that I had caused. That psychology degree and a *lot* of prayers helped me to stop being a mean and bitter person toward others—and a lot of times, I had been mean for no apparent reason, except that hurt people, *hurt people*. I knew I didn't want to be like my father, still belittling people and being so negative. Thank God for changing me! It feels better to be genuinely kind and nice to people.

Oh, but I didn't stop there! I was just getting started. My petty ass found the email address of that student services counselor from Everest, and I sent her a copy of my conferred degree from Liberty and thanked her for making me challenge myself. The fact that she had told me not to switch from an associate's to a bachelor's degree meant that I needed to prove to her that she was wrong. Baby, after earning my bachelor's degree at LU, I reenrolled there and completed a master's of arts in human services degree. And my GPA that time was 3.53!

I was happy because my mother could attend my graduation ceremony this time. She had not been able to attend my high school graduation, because she had suffered second- and third-degree burns and was in the ICU burn unit at the time; she couldn't leave the hospital, although she wanted to. My mother cried back then, because she really wanted to be there, and I told her it was okay because she was there in spirit. I gave my cap and gown, my high school diploma, my love, and my efforts all to my mom.

Lynchburg was an experience, honey, because we were not used to those dang mountains. Graduation day was hot! The sun was sunning! Our guest speaker was Mitt Romney, and an airplane kept flying over our ceremony. I thought it was rude, and I started canvassing the area around me. I could see Mitt's security team perched on top of different buildings, looking like snipers. We were safe; at least I felt like we were.

My parents, two of my father's sisters (Auntie Dot: loud and hilarious as usual and Auntie Gent: softer spoken, but could get loud), and my cousin Bernard (Nard was my hype man cousin who could out-shout a marching band) were there at my graduation. Bernard was yelling my name so loudly; he made me feel like a celebrity that day! My mother's auntie (who my mom is named after—my sweet great-auntie Sarah) was there, and another cousin named Tavares (my mother's sister's only son) was there with his wife, Joanne. Meanwhile, I was still in shock. I couldn't believe that I was about to graduate from what I classified as a *real* university. I had finally fulfilled my desire to have a college education.

# After Graduation

I started working as a mental health professional for a company that was supposed to be providing specific services to children and adolescents. I took my job seriously, but apparently the company did not. At some point the state fined them, and the fines kept piling up. Eventually, that company went out of business. I was troubled by the abrupt closure, because I had just purchased a brand-new Honda CR-V that had only five miles on it when I drove it off the lot.

I figured I could run an ethical business and pay off my car loan. My commute from Charlotte to Rock Hill wasn't long, so I found an office space and signed a lease for it. I had clients who were ready to receive the mental health services that I was prepared to offer, but I had to wait for a decision from the State of South Carolina on whether it would allow businesses like mine to operate. While I waited, I registered my business's name (Humble Beginnings) with the state, got my National Provider Identifier (NPI), which is a 10-digit ID number for health care providers, and I created care plans for the clients that I was preparing to work with.

Then, the decision came: South Carolina had decided that no new mental health businesses could operate unless they were a licensed medical doctor to authorize visits with clients. That was a hard blow! The one time that I had the courage to go into business for myself, I got slapped in the face with a big fat *no*!

The devil was trying to convince me that the Lord didn't want me to be great. In the words Mr. Brown, one of the characters from Tyler Perry's universe, "The devil is a liar!" But I couldn't seem to shake the feeling of being abandoned and alone. No one could understand what was going through my mind. But! What I learned from that experience is that sometimes God puts us in places *alone* because He needs us to realize that we do *not* need anybody but Him! Amen! I'm not going to lie; it was hard work trying to convince myself that God had doors that would open for me. I even felt embarrassed, because my sister and my parents had gone with me to see the office that I'd picked out, and my father was taking measurements because he was ready to come in and make the place feel like my own.

I was starting to feel the familiar *You're a failure* thought seep in. I reminded myself that South Carolina's decision was not based on anything I had or had not done. The decision was based on companies who had severely damaged the state's systems. I wasn't about to lose the first brand-new car I'd ever owned, so I figured it wouldn't hurt if I applied to some temporary staffing agencies for work. Thank God I got an instant response! I accepted a role as a temporary human resources associate for a company that was near the Charlotte Douglas airport.

Around the time I took on this new gig, I met a dishonest dude on a social media platform.

# The Dude From Social Media

One day, out of nowhere, a guy sent me a friend request on social media. He and I had *one* mutual friend, and that person wasn't really a friend of mine; we just so happened to have grown up in the same neighborhood.

One mutual friend should have been an indicator to not accept his friend request.

But! I wanted a travel partner, and in all honesty, I was lonely.

He wasn't my type, because I was a bit taller than him, he had a receding hairline, he smoked cigarettes, and he drank alcohol. Plus, he wasn't the sharpest knife in the drawer… and ladies, I've seen egg rolls with more length than his tiny baby carrot.

On July 12, 2015, the mutual friend sent me a direct message saying, "Congratulations to u and the Social Media Dude's happiness."

"Thank you," I replied.

But I'm guessing she was disturbed by what she had seen on the platform, because she messaged me again, writing, "He is a nice/ sweet guy… we was just together memorial day at the beach but never thought he would date one of my friends…"

I wrote back, "He is indeed a very nice guy & he shared with me the reason he had initially unfriended me & I learned a LOT of things that I didn't know about myself that you had allegedly said… one of your friends? I am an associate of yours & only know of you from the neighborhood we grew up in… yes, we are 'friends' on this platform, but nothing more than that… have a good evening girl."

According to the Social Media Dude, she'd told him that I used to steal the guys she dated away from her when we were younger. Or something to that effect.

First of all, she was like a grade or two higher than I was, so the only time I'd ever interacted with her was… never!

I mean, I saw her on the school bus, but it wasn't like we hung out, or like we were ever friends.

Besides, I wasn't even allowed to go beyond my front porch, and I certainly wasn't allowed to have a boyfriend until I turned 17! I had graduated high school by then, so I debunked her lies.

Why did I disregard that particular red flag, though?

My goodness, I ignored the fact that I knew I didn't like drama, and proceeded with blinders on.

Our first trip together should have been our last.

We had driven down to Myrtle Beach for the Fourth of July weekend. He'd parked his car at my parents' home, and we left in my CR-V. I exited the neighborhood from the end that had us closest to WT Harris Boulevard. When I turned onto Markway, there was a bicycle inner tube lying in the road. His mind convinced him that he saw a black snake, and he started screaming and hollering at the top of his lungs! His legs were moving like he was running; he was hitting the dashboard with one hand and holding on to the door with the other hand. I laughed until I cried.

"Hell no!" he screamed. "Keep driving! Get me the hell away from that goddamn snake!"

I had to slow down, because there was no way that I could drive while laughing so hard. He was livid with me because I was laughing.

"Hell, I'm afraid of snakes, too," I told him, "but that is not a snake, and therefore, you are funny."

His attitude was on a thousand! He said in the snarkiest voice, "Well, what is it then, Miss Know-It-All?"

"It is a bicycle inner tube," I said. "Would you like for me to pick it up and show you?"

My oh my, if looks could kill. LMBO.

We got to dirty Myrtle Beach and couldn't find a reasonably priced hotel, being that it was Fourth of July weekend. I had tried to tell him that he wouldn't be able to find a hotel that was reasonably priced, but he didn't want to listen.

So, basically, we took a trip to the beach to turn right TF back around, and checked in to a hotel in Charlotte. TF!

Also, he got mad because I wouldn't allow him to fondle me while I was driving—weird. It was the first time that I realized something was not right about him, because he wanted to argue constantly. He even told me that it was healthy to argue in a relationship.

What? It's healthy? Says who?

I was so glad when that weekend came to an end.

He halfway apologized to me for his demeanor, and when he came to visit again, he had a bouquet of yellow roses for my mother and a bouquet for me. Nice gesture, I suppose.

Our next trip was to Atlanta to celebrate his birthday, because he had never gone there before.

Let me tell you, we argued damn near the whole way there and back to Charlotte. I couldn't pinpoint what set him off, but it was like he enjoyed having anger issues.

I hated putting on a fake smile to take pictures with him. I was miserable with him!

While we were in Atlanta, we went to the World of Coca-Cola. My sister had asked him to bring her back a souvenir from there. After all, she called him brother-in-law, even though we never considered marriage. He pretended to not have money and asked me to pay for it, and said he'd pay me back. What I learned from that Virgo was not to trust him with repayment, because in his words, "As long as I owe you, you'll never go broke."

Red flag number 999!

Later, my sister's gift purchase turned into an argument, because I asked him for my money. I mean, *I see you spending cash in this store. Hell, I wear glasses, but I ain't damned blind!*

I was exhausted at the amount of effort he put into arguing, and made up my mind that when we returned to Charlotte, I was going to be done with him.

Funny how persuasive people with motives can be.

Dysfunction seemed to be at the center of my life, no matter which way I turned.

We stopped at Arby's on our way back to Charlotte, and I finally understood why his demeanor was so inconsistent. While we were seated at a table, he admitted to me that he had a cocaine addiction. He said something in reference to his getting sober and asked what my sentiments were.

I stated that I wished him the best, but that was not good enough for him.

He pushed the rhetorical button and asked if I thought he'd stay sober.

"No," I said honestly.

He let out a long, dramatic, "Wooooooww! Thanks for believing in me. See, that's the problem with a lot of Black women."

Before he could breathe another word, I got up from the table and went to use the restroom. I stayed in there for a very long time, praying and asking God to remove me from this drama, because I hated it.

I did not hate him. I hated the unnecessary drama he created.

About a month after the Atlanta trip, the regular football season was finally upon us! I predicted the Carolina Panthers would go to the Super Bowl. Went! Haters were saying we wouldn't win. We didn't, and you know what? I don't care what anyone says… I will always believe that Super Bowl L (50) was rigged to keep Cam Newton from earning the team's first ring. I surely did. I said what I said! We had a beautiful 15–1 season, and it felt like pure destiny. Cam was doing his thing, dabbing. Hell, he even had my mama dabbing! Our defense was terrorizing all opponents, and our whole city was lit up! Then, here comes the night we had all been anticipating. And just like that… the floor dropped out. The Broncos won the game, 24–10. I was proud of the season and proud of the team. I also felt gutted, because our ending didn't match the story we were living.

The same concept applied to the Social Media Dude. The story we were living in front of people did not match our chaotic reality.

Valentine's Day came, and he got me a Snoopy stuffed animal (because I love Snoopy). It was inside of a sturdy wicker basket, and the base of the basket was filled with miniature Snickers bars. He also got me flowers and balloons.

A very lovely day, right?

Manipulation? Perhaps.

My gift to him was a trip to Myrtle Beach the following month. I had a Hilton Grand Vacation package that needed to be used, so I figured, *Why not go to the beach?* I also presented a cruise to him for his birthday later in the year.

Calm down!

I know what you're probably thinking, but hear me out.

I had never been on an airplane before, and since he said he wasn't afraid of flying, that meant I would have someone to accompany me on my first flight to Miami for the cruise. And he had never cruised before, so I guess I accommodated him? Now, I knew good and hell well that I had cruise credits that needed to be used, or else I'd lose my money. He accepted the gift, and I booked the cruise to the Bahamas for his birthday in 2016.

In Myrtle Beach, he wanted to buy a timeshare.

I knew damn well I was not about to get caught up in owning property with him. His credit was pitiful!

The salesperson was very pushy, and convinced the Social Media Dude to accept the package.

A part of the gimmick was, if a customer did not have enough cash for a down payment, which they likely wouldn't have, then the salesperson would sign them up for a Hilton Honors American Express card.

Well, they ran his credit, and his application was immediately declined.

I thought I saw smoke coming out of the computer at one point.

For shits and giggles, I allowed them to run my credit… and the credit line was significant!

My crazy ass added him to my credit card account, trying to help him build his credit. He ran up that damn American Express bill, but I politely cut his ass off! And then, he had the whole audacity to cop an attitude anytime I asked for the nearly $3,000 he owed me for everything he had charged on my card. Did he repay me? What did I tell you that I learned about that particular Virgo?

He thought he was going to show off in front of his family with the American Express, but I went into the app and deactivated his card! We had gone to Charleston for his sister's graduation, and before we went, he'd had the audacity to tell me how to conduct myself.

The master of chaos had told me not to curse in front of them, and I snapped back! I told him, "Unlike you, I know how to conduct myself in the company of others." I wanted that weekend to be over the same day we got on the road for Charleston!

In part of our trip, we were sightseeing, and we passed by Emanuel AME Zion Church—the same church where several parishioners were killed during Bible study, a little over a year earlier. We had just left a seafood restaurant, and I was sick to my stomach. I really do not care for seafood, but I'd tried to eat it anyway. My stomach felt like I had been on a drunken spree.

Why did I keep thinking things would get better with each vacation? They were all disasters because of his mood swings.

Later that year, we arrived in Miami for the cruise.

*Horrible* trip. WTH was I thinking?

He was broke, with nothing in his pockets but lint! Who in their right mind goes out of the country with no money?

He kept leaving the cabin after I had showered and lain down for the evening. One of those times when he left, I took some money out of my purse, crumpled it up, and placed it on the floor where he'd see it. When he spotted it, he snatched it up really quick. Then a look of being chastised appeared on his face. His moral compass allowed him the decency to ask if the money was mine.

I acted like I didn't know it was there and said, "What money?"

He pointed to the spot and said, "The money was right there on the floor."

"I left when you did," I said, "and when I came back, I wasn't looking at the floor. I was looking at this good ol' bed." I knew that if he had money in his pockets, he'd leave the cabin. I didn't feel like arguing anymore. I told him that housekeeping probably had come in while we were out.

"That's what they asses get," he said. "Sneaking in people's rooms when they not in it. They dropped they damn money!"

After the cruise was over and our airplane landed at Charlotte Douglas, I was ready to walk home, I did not want to hear his voice any longer!

It sounded like you asked, "Did you argue?"

Did we!

I was legit through this time. I couldn't deal with his inconsistent moods. I promised to God in heaven that I was done with him. The feeling was mutual this time, though. Most likely because he wanted to dip without repaying his debt.

Too much of my time had been wasted with him, and it was time that I really focused more on me. I had to.

But riddle me this: How in the hell had I completed studies for a psychology degree, only to allow a bumpkin to work my last good nerve?

After that hot mess, I vowed to myself that I would never settle again. I understand my value, and I know my worth.

I found me!

I would rather treat myself to a solo lunch and a solo trip than deal with foolery like that ever again!

Then one day, all of a sudden and out of the blue, I get a direct message on social media: "Hello Angela."

He knew I hated being called by my legal name, and I was in no mood to mince words.

"Any idea when you'll be able to make a payment?" I wrote back.

"Huh?" he replied.

"American Express," I fired back.

This son of a biscuit eater then wrote, "Oh you on that again hmmm I guess cause you call me petty."

I was pissed! I said, "No. I guess because you owe $2,700. You act like I'm not supposed to ask for what you owe!"

"Have you paid your part yet?" that bitch said.

What damn difference did it make if I had paid my part or not? Nigga! Pay me WTF you owe me, period!

My blood pressure was elevated at that point.

It annoyed me even more that he was acting like he hadn't been confronted about repaying me, because his shrimp-dick-ass said, "What's my chance of seeing you?"

Call me the Wicked Witch of the West! I waited until the following day and replied, "Good morning. It's a great day to be alive. TO AN-SWER YOUR QUESTION: Your chances of seeing me, are as great as mine are, with getting the money you owe me!"

I figured maybe I should be nice. After all, I needed help driving up to Virginia to look at a university I was considering. He agreed to go along to help me drive, and I let him know that I was not going to party, because I had to be present for the tasks that I would be there to complete. I already knew that it was going to be chaotic! I allowed him to sleep while I drove us to Virginia, and the agreement was he'd drive back.

Virginia Beach was cool, but the school wasn't for me. So it was time to head back to Charlotte — and what do you know? Here came the jackassery. I mean, he was pouting like a toddler that had never been disciplined.

"You must don't care that I have to get back to see about my mama," he said to me.

I looked at that pathetic being and reminded him that he'd said he would drive back, since I'd driven the whole way up. I gently said to him, "You are the holdup. You can't drive from the outside of the passenger's side."

I know he was sick of me, because he was slamming my car's doors and driving erratically.

I didn't open my mouth. Didn't say a word.

He had already proven to me that I could not trust him, because he'd get upset at me for the things *he* said and did. That's how manipulators operate. He would flip the script, he would disrespect me, then act offended when I responded. Confusion was part of the control he thought he had. Manipulators want the freedom to hurt people without responsibility. He wanted me quiet so that he could stay comfortable and keep pretending he was innocent. The audacity!

On that drive home, the argument had already manifested in his mind, so I beat him to the punch and said, "If I'm responding, you get mad. If I am silent, you get mad. It's beyond the point where I am able to funnel energy into situations that are not beneficial. I am tired of arguing and being ridiculed. I am not ignoring you and being antisocial; I am being protective of my feelings, my dignity, and my harmony. If I'm not able to be in good spirits, then I'd rather sit back and chill. The thing you don't seem to understand is that words cannot be taken back after they have been spoken. And a lot of times, those words are very painful and can damage the mind, break the heart, and create distance between people."

"Okay, I understand," he said. Lies!

We finally made it to my neighborhood, and he was still driving like a wild man. It was truly pissing me off. I told him if he damaged my car, he was going to pay to repair it.

"You wanna bet?" he said.

"Eat a dick!" I told him. I was so angry.

"I don't eat dick!" he said. "I eat pussy."

"And you don't do that too well," I said. "Hell, how long were we together? Out of all that time, I only climaxed once! Your services are no longer needed!"

# Celibacy

After I broke up with the Social Media Dude in 2016, my focus was solely on reclaiming my body, my peace, my boundaries, and my dignity. After all the dysfunction I had allowed in my life, I needed to take back what the devil had stolen from me. (Or had I given it to him?) Dysfunction was the main reason I ignored the advances of the "florist" who was coming on to me. *Mr. Weedman Florist Sir, I have money to pay for my ganja; I'm not dividing the pie for some damn weed!* Who does that? I am sure some people would, but not me. I care too much about my well-being. Besides, he had a whole entire woman already! I kept telling him I didn't have time for no Jerry Springer shit in my life!

I knew my value. I understood my worth. I wasn't giving my body to anyone. Celibacy, for me, is a decision, a boundary, a shift, a stance, a season, a commitment, a pivot — not a practice session. And I wasn't going to change that for some two-timing florist.

Perhaps he thought I was kidding, because he texted me, "U cute."

The florist was texting me like he was writing a message on those Sweethearts Valentine's candies. I wasn't in the mood, so I texted back and asked straight up, "Sooooo um… are you actually single?"

"No," he said honestly.

"Well… what are you doing?" I wrote back. I had already been a mistress, and I was not about to revisit that situation with anyone else.

"I wanted to c u," he replied. Bold.

I'm looking at the phone like, *Who ties your shoestrings for you? Because you obviously have not heard what I said.* With all the sass, I responded to his text saying, "Why is that? You're not a single man, and I'm not in the business of being a side chick. I'm just trying to get gas is all."

He did apologize, although he didn't mean it, because he started flirting again. Eventually, I just quit responding and held on to the flowers that I had until I found a new florist to supply my bouquets. I was in no hurry to find a new one, though. I needed to see about my health, because my doctor had recently told me that I had to have surgery.

In 2018, I learned that I had a uterine fibroid, which had been growing.

Prior to the surgery, the doctor reminded me to not be sexually active for a specified period of time. And I reminded her that I was still celibate. She said, "Just so you know, when you do become active, you may still be able to get pregnant, because you still have your ovaries. In the event that you become pregnant, you wouldn't be able to carry it, though, because you will no longer have a uterus." I mean, I had intentionally never in my life been pregnant, so who was going to get me pregnant now? Casper? The friendly ghost?

I had to sign an agreement and a waiver indicating that I understood what she'd explained to me.

I was supposed to be a patient of Novant Hospital for two days, but I ended up being there for a whole week, because apparently you cannot leave the hospital without passing gas. The day of surgery, I was petrified, because I was reminded that there was the possibility of death during the procedure. I was okay until death became a reality for me. I didn't tell anyone, though. I didn't want them panicked or overly worried about me. I was thankful that my sister was there and would not leave my side. My really close friend, Audrey was there, too. Even though she had her own medical issues, she told me, "I have to be there for my Angie."

My cousins Vern and Quinetta (who we called Netta—Netta is Tavares' sister), and Joanne (Netta's sister-in-law) were there as well. When the patient care technician called my name, we all stood and held hands. I led us into prayer, and Vern walked with me as they wheeled me to the area for surgery prep. Vern told me, "Bye, Angie." I remembered my grandfather telling me once that goodbye meant forever, and that's exactly what I told her.

"I will see you later," I told her. "This is not goodbye."

From the time I met the anesthesiologist to the time that I was being wheeled to the door or an elevator, I was out like a light! When I awakened, I was in a room, asking, "Where am I?"

My sister Tonya was lying in a padded nook taking a nap.

I felt like I had been bar-hopping and was very queasy.

To help with healing, I forced myself to get out of that hospital bed and walk down different halls. I was hoping my walks would make gas move, but I wasn't eating the hospital's food. My sister would look at the menu and see what she wanted, and I'd order it for her. I was on a low-carb diet, and even the eggs were awful. I asked for a protein shake along with the meals, and the staff obliged.

The day that the ice cream guy was making room calls, I asked for some chocolate ice cream. I don't know what it was about chocolate, but it could always make me release flatulence.

My friend Vee came to visit me—I always called her "Vee," because her full name took too long to say. Back in the '90s when I was Electric Sliding at Betty's Place, our favorite club at the time, Vee was right there sliding right along with me. At some point, our friendship lost its momentum, and my ability to be nice to people was not fully established back then. Now, in my hospital room, I apologized to her for all the mean things I had ever said to hurt her. She told me I didn't owe her an apology.

"Please let me say what I need to say," I told her. I was speaking from a healed heart and mind. I fell asleep after she left, and around four o'clock the next morning, I pressed the nurse's call button and told them I was ready to go home, because I'd finally released some gas. It was like I had hit the jackpot!

I took maybe two of the Dilaudid pills the doctor had prescribed.

Dilaudid is such a strong opioid that there was no way I was going to swallow another one! I did not like the effects of the pills. They made me feel like I had no control over my body.

I decided to use nature's medicine. Ganja. And I had found a new florist. But I cut him off quickly, too. He sent me a dick pic without my even asking for it. I mean, he was the same length and width of an Aquafina water bottle, but it was disrespectful as hell to send me a photo of it!

He also had a girlfriend or wife. I did purchase some flowers from him before cutting him off though.

The ganja helped with the pain. Still, whenever I'd cough, I could feel the tightening in my bikini area.

My sister was faithful. She helped me to get into the shower, she made sure I had my protein drinks, and she talked nonstop.

I had a cruise planned for later that year. I was glad to have the surgery behind me, because it meant that I wouldn't be on the cruise worrying about having to shower and change clothes four or five times a day. It was my first time going to Cozumel, Mexico, and it definitely was not my last. This time, I got blunts on the ship by wrapping them and putting them inside of my sock, making sure my sneaker was tied tight! I sold a few blunts, and one girl said to me "Damn! This is loud. You don't have anything else?" I laughed like hell, because *Miss Lil Ma'am Lady, what? This cabin is not a dispensary, so I only have what I just bought in Miami.* I made back the money I spent to purchase the bag, and made sure everyone on the trip with me had their own blunt. A really good time was had. Honey, Cozumel owed us nothing! We partied so much.

The end of 2018 was upon us, and I got a phone call stating that Audrey had passed away. I cried inconsolably. She'd been like a sister to me. Being blood relations couldn't have made us any closer. I met Audrey through her sister, Joanne. Audrey was such a loving person. Sometimes she could be mean, but for the most part, she was kind and sweet. Audrey and I talked on the phone every night when she got off work and settled in. I wanted to make sure she'd gotten home okay, and she would tell me about her day. She was a cook at the Waffle House, so she saw a little bit of everything, and there was always a story to be told.

When I was asked to assist with writing her obituary and to share some joyful remarks, I didn't think twice about it. "Of course I'll do it," I said. I am not a public speaker, so I wrote what I wanted to say, and practiced. I tried to speak without crying. I was honored to speak at her service, and I told everyone about the time she'd gone on her first and only cruise with Joanne, Quinetta, and me, in 2010. Anyone who knew Audrey knew that she'd curse you out and tell you she loved you in the same sentence. I was so honored that one of my former co-workers (who could praise the Lord like no other) Erika Dooley (now Brooks), played her violin selections during Audrey's services. When I tell you Erika is a beast on that violin!

As I listened to Erika play the violin selections, my mind took me back to how I had pulled out every trick I had trying to convince Audrey to go on that 2010 cruise. That was a challenge all by itself. She had every excuse known to man, but the main one was because the *Titanic* had sunk. I understood her fear of the unknown, so I told her, "God did not give us the spirit of fear." I think that was the line that finally pushed her to say yes. It was her first cruise, and the funniest part is that when we got back to the Port of Miami, Audrey didn't even want to get off the ship. We had a ball, and that was the memory I wanted everyone to hold on to when I spoke—she was afraid, but she did it anyway.

After my partial hysterectomy, I told myself that I'd remain celibate. I'd been celibate since breaking up with the Social Media Dude back in 2016. But hear me clearly: Celibacy, when a woman chooses it, is never just about closing her legs. It's about *opening her life*. It's a whole internal shift—spiritual, emotional, mental, and relational. It's a reclamation, not a restriction. When I decided to be celibate, I was doing far more than declining sex. I was reclaiming my peace. I was no longer letting chaos, confusion, or half-hearted connections into my body or my spirit. I was reestablishing boundaries. I was choosing who gets access—and who doesn't. And that boundary was about my whole self, not just my physical body.

Celibacy was also about resetting my mind. Celibacy often comes with clarity. I started seeing people's intentions faster. I stopped negotiating with red flags. I *stopped confusing attention with affection*. Celibacy allowed me to heal from old wounds. This space was different, but it allowed me to unlearn patterns and detach from past entanglements, and rebuild trust with myself. I decided that when I was ready to reconnect, it would be with a purpose.

With sex off the table, the distractions fell away. I began focusing on calling, creativity, and alignment. My energy shifted. My discernment sharpened. I told myself that I would raise my standards to where they should have been all along. Celibacy kept me honest and true to myself, because any man that wanted to "get to know me" had to show up with something deeper than desire. This allowed me to filter out the unserious, the inconsistent, and the spiritually malnourished. Choosing myself over validation was not about deprivation—it was about elevation. It was me saying, "I'm worth more than momentary comfort."

Celibacy is a whole lifestyle, a whole mindset, and a whole spiritual pivot. It wasn't about me saying no to sex. It was about me saying yes to myself.

# The Confrontation

In June of 2020, spoke on the phone with my sister to let her know the issues I was now facing with our father. I couldn't begin to fathom when he had developed a lustful eye for me, but it was giving weird energy. I asked her to be with me for moral support while I confronted him. I scheduled the day for her and my oldest brother to come to my parents' house (I'd been residing at my parents' home since moving back to Charlotte in 2010). Tonya ended up being a no-show; however, my brother showed up.

I had carefully planned what I wanted to say and even written it down. I sat beside my brother and began to read. I said:

"I will start by saying how much it saddens me that I even have to put my thoughts on paper to address you. Over the past two to three months, you have made me feel extremely uncomfortable. I have kept my mouth closed for about as long as I can. You constantly walk up on me when I'm in the kitchen, in a very inappropriate way!"

My father looked like he was about to say something, so I continued quickly:

"Hold up! Before you deny anything, rethink your actions and do not make a victim feel like the suspect. To your credit, I can say that you have not laid a hand on me, but the fact that you get creepily close to me is uncalled for! Your defense for issues when you do not want to face the truth is, 'I don't remember.' I challenge that response with: Whether you remember or not does not mean it never happened. Sometimes I think back to when we lived on Purser, Mama and me was watching a movie on Lifetime, and you just so happened to be there that Saturday. I do not remember the name of the movie, but it was about a woman

"

who had been raped. And I said, 'I don't like watching movies like that, because it reminds me of when I got raped.' Your response to me as my father was, 'Well what were you wearing that caused it?' I never forgot your words, because they weren't the words of a protector; they were the words of an accuser. It shouldn't have mattered if I walked around wearing nothing but a bright yellow wig. It was uncalled for, for me to be raped by one of your friends! What was I wearing? That is the most insensitive thing anyone could ever say to a victim! You asking me that is the same as me trying to make a racist white person understand what Black Lives Matter actually means. But that's not the true reason why I am writing this letter. I should have corrected you that day when you said to me, 'You bout finished, bae?' *First of all, I am not your bae! Your wife, my mother, is and should be your bae! I am your daughter! That is all and nothing more!* I don't even cook anymore because you make me so uncomfortable! You walk up on me like you are confused, but you know what you are doing because you have done it more than once. And no I most certainly am not imagining things, because you most definitely are creepy and make me uncomfortable being around you! For you to sit and watch me when I am walking is disgusting. How dare you tell me that my butt bounces when I walk. Seriously, like what kind of father does that? And people wonder why you and me do not have a strong father-daughter bond, and they are even more surprised when I correct them and let them know I am by no means a daddy's girl. You had people believing I was spoiled by you… but the truth is I was traumatized the majority of my life by you."

I never wavered in what I said. I didn't make eye contact with him because he was looking down into his hands. I continued reading, "When I am in the kitchen, there is literally no reason for you to be as close as you are to me, and it makes me feel threatened. It is beyond embarrassing and sickening that I have to put my thoughts into words. I said something to Mama when I first noticed your behavior, and I begged her not to say anything to you. But think for a minute how your wife, my mother, felt hearing me tell the truth on a perverted man, her husband. I wanted to make 100 percent sure that I was not imagining things. I even quit smoking weed for several days, so that I would not have a clouded judgment! You literally walked up on me like some dude in the streets trying to get with me! I was really pissed off by your inappropriate actions, and remembered all of the other reasons you've given me to dislike you. You are my dad! I don't know how you got in your mind that it would go beyond that, but rest assured, that cannot and will not ever happen! I hate having to feel like I am going to have to defend myself against you. I am so disappointed in you."

I don't know if he paid attention the whole time, because when he stood up, he told my brother he was ready to be taken to the store. I looked at my brother like *WTF?*

"Hold up, Dad," my brother said. "You're not going to address what she said?"

My father shrugged his shoulders, got up, and went into the kitchen, crying.

*What in the entire hell? How are you the one crying when you're the reason for the chaos?*

In that moment, I found myself pushing through memories that still had teeth.

***

My father and I may not always see eye to eye on things, but best believe, I'm gonna have his back!

Here's a prime example. He had driven me to the dentist in the spring of 2021, because I was unsure if I'd be sedated or not. Turns out, sedation was not needed.

After leaving the dentist's office, we stopped at a convenience store on the way home. It had a Subway inside. My father went inside to play his numbers along with my mom's, and I went to Subway to get everyone's food.

When I got to the counter, I heard the cashier saying something slick to the elderly Black lady that was ahead of us. I kept my mouth closed and minded my business.

My father got up to the register with a lot of cards to play his and Mama's numbers. Okay. The cashier shooed him like he was a damn horsefly! She told him, "You gone have to move to the side and wait, because I got other customers to tend to."

She didn't know who she'd just gotten slick with!

I walked up to that short, round, palm-colored girl with a look that let her know that shit could easily be rearranged in that store!

I looked her in her eyes and said, "I do beg your finest pardon?" She huffed.

"Hold up," I said. "Hold the fuck up! Whatchu not gone do."

That heffa rolled her eyes!

"See," I continued. "I should've got in yo ass when you got slick at the mouth with this lady over here. This man right here! Bitch! This is my father, and I will be damned if your li'l stumpy ass is going to disrespect him! Not on my damn watch."

She reared back like she was about that life!

"You were the one who applied for this job, so you knew customer service was involved when you accepted the job offer," I told her. "If you're not in the mood to provide customer service, this ain't the job for you!"

"Say that shit sis!" someone behind us said.

"I know that shit right!" someone else said "You tell her!"

"You don't know me," I continued, "but let me assure you, at any given time you'd like to step from behind that register, please do. There's nothing between us but air and opportunity."

She sucked her teeth, adjusted her dirty blonde hair, and said with an attitude, "Excuse me!"

I may not have been given the best life by my father, but I don't play about him or my mother!

After that incident, I went to Walgreens to pick up some medicine and just so happened to see the elderly lady whom I'd had the honor of defending at the convenience store, the one the cashier had gotten slick with.

"I thank God for running into you again," she said to me. "Thank you for taking up and speaking up for me earlier. That girl is always mean like that."

I smiled and said, "I thank God that I was able to be there for you. I hate seeing people disrespect their elders, because that's not how I was raised. I get that some elders are mean and rude, but you were not. You didn't say anything to that girl. She made me hot!"

She reached out her arms and asked if she could give me a hug.

I pray that that little elderly lady is doing well, if she's still among the living.

Speaking of among the living, my heart broke when I got the news in November 2021 that Mrs. Jackson had passed away. I remember standing in shock saying, "My Mrs. Jackson?" I was in disbelief.

I never deleted her number from my contacts.

Being that the man from California had known Mrs. Jackson, I called him to tell him about her passing. A recording played, saying that his phone had been disconnected and was no longer in service.

Being that his drug of choice was alcohol, his phone would sometimes be turned off and he wouldn't know it, because he'd drink himself into a stupor.

Just then, I remembered that he'd given me his pastor's phone number so that the pastor could get in contact with him to let him know to pay his bill.

"Hello," I texted the pastor. "My name is Angie. I am a friend of the man from California. I am trying to get in touch with him to let him know something important."

My phone rang.

It was the pastor. He introduced himself and said, "Hey. I don't know how to tell you this, but he passed away in February of 2020."

I was silent.

I didn't know if I should feel numb or not.

I really didn't know how to explain what I felt.

I suddenly heard myself gasp.

I was crying.

He'd been so mean to me.

Why was I crying?

I apologized to the pastor and told him that I needed a moment and that I'd call him back. After I got myself together and returned the call, he let me know that the man from California had died of natural causes.

May 24, 2022

I have never been a gym rat, but my presence at the gym had become fairly strong, and in the spring of 2022, I began making new acquaintances. One of the people who made the strongest impression on me was Carlene Moore-Tyson, she was solid in her Christian faith, and I admired that about her. She claimed me as her adoptive daughter, and she spoke a prophecy over my life. At that point, I had never mentioned a word to her about the three prophecies I'd gotten when I was a Florida resident. I'd even see Diontez (my former coworker) at the gym occasionally. Diontez's desk was beside mine, when we worked for Walmart Corporate. He would have a Scripture for me every day… it may not have been an actual Scripture from any version of the Bible, which made it funnier. That is how I came to call him Pastuh. I had to make Pastuh a homemade banana pudding for his birthday and told him he'd better be at the gym every day to work it off.

Carlene and I developed a bond, and she became someone that I could trust my deepest secrets with. Most of the secrets, you've already read about by now. She kept speaking a prophecy over me, and I eventually told her what other people had told me. In that moment, she touched and agreed with their messages and began praying for the Lord to keep me covered with His divine protection. She asked the Lord to bless her to see the day when all the prophecies had come to pass.

Carlene, a mother, saw something in me that I didn't recognize in myself. Call it mother's intuition, but here I am writing the very book that she and others had prophesied.

Thank you, Carlene. I honor you far more than just as a gym acquaintance. You are someone who saw me, claimed me, prayed over me, and believed in my calling.

For several weeks leading up to May 24, I tried countless times to get in contact with my sister, Tonya. I knew that she was battling an addiction, but this time, her distance felt different. In a dream that I had—this is where being a seer terrifies me—we were at a restaurant, eating, laughing, and reminiscing. All of a sudden, the lights went out. I heard her say, "Ahhh shit! The feds are about to raid this place!" Then there was complete silence. I started calling her name, and at first, she laughed and said, "What, pig? You scared, baby?" It felt cold in that place, then somehow, we were outside, where it was misty. Not a steady rain, and it was foggy. I can still see this dream very vividly. All of a sudden, I heard something fall. I couldn't see what it was, but I kept yelling, "Tonya!" I was actually talking in my sleep, because I woke myself up when I said her name.

I never deleted my call log with her. On April 26, I called her, and she let the phone ring once and then declined the call.

May 4, sent to voicemail. So, I called right back. Sent to voicemail again.

I wanted to hear her voice, because that dream still had me shook. I called her again on May 16, and my call was declined again.

After church one Sunday, I texted her pictures that I'd taken of her. I was elated when she responded! She wrote, "Yeah honey beautiful now skinny as hell."

"You're still beautiful!" I replied, without missing a beat.

"It's the Queen day well tks," she texted back.

I was elated to be texting with my sister, but our dialogue still felt so distant. I texted back to her, "& is. You're welcome." I sent her some pictures of a time we had gone to The Cheesecake Factory; we had gone to celebrate life. She ordered a gigantic burrito, and I had warned her before she got it that it was huge and she wasn't going to be able to consume it all. But she damn sure tried! The food won, of course. I ordered a slice of lemon meringue cheesecake, and the first bite tasted like love.

"Ah. Chile bye! It ain't that doggone good!" Tonya said to me.

"How much you wanna bet?" I said. I slid the plate over to her, and she became animated. The way she called the waiter to our table… oh my goodness, she had folks in there laughing.

Now, I added a text with those pictures and wrote, "I tried to tell you, you couldn't eat all of that big ass burrito lmbo!"

"I know right it was good though," she responded.

I knew that she was babysitting for one of our cousins, so when my phone rang after one o'clock in the morning, I ignored it. Then I got a text that said, "AWCZG AZ D aegwu7DVD sqyfq66YE3w211 xQ4@ n 1q¹1t/-8 54daqd51qxra¹1 a 35." I ignored that as well, because I thought perhaps the little one that she was babysitting had her phone, and was playing with it.

Except.

At 1:39 a.m., I got another text that said, "Hello my name is Maurice."

That dream started replaying in my mind. All I could see was darkness, even though I had sat up on the side of my bed and turned on my lamp.

The next text came at 1:40 a.m. and said, "I'm not exactly sure who you are or how you know Latonya but she is in the hospital in ICU."

I gasped for air. I reached for my asthma pump. My hands were shaking; my head was throbbing. I put on my housecoat, grabbed my car keys, and let my parents know that I was going to the hospital to see about Tonya. When I parked my car, I got another call from my sister's phone. The voice on the phone told me that she'd gotten a hold of some drugs that were laced with fentanyl. He said she'd passed out for a while and that he'd been afraid to call the police. All I was hearing was negligence. How long had my sister gone without oxygen? I snapped! I told him to meet me at the hospital because I was beating his ass on sight! I called a lot of contacts in my phone.

When I got to my sister's hospital room, I saw my sister lying there with wires attached to her scalp. The nurse was applying more. I asked her what she was doing.

"This is to monitor brain activity, because we don't know how long she was without oxygen," the nurse responded.

I fucking lost it! I broke down. I was angry at this Maurice person. I was even angrier at my sister for allowing her addiction to take over her life.

"So, my sister is brain-dead?" I asked the nurse.

"Well…" she said.

"I know there are things you are limited to saying," I told her. "Tell me this, how many times have you seen a person in this condition recover?"

She shook her head no. "I'm so sorry," she said. "I have never seen it."

Someone posted my sister's death on social media *before* I was ready to announce it to the world! Then, out of nowhere, I got a call though the Messenger app. It was from someone who had grown up with us. She was the girl who enjoyed drama. I ignored her call, because I'll bet you a dollar to a doughnut, she just wanted to know what had happened. I hadn't heard from her in years! She was messy when we were children, and was still messy as an adult.

My mind went back to the time when the girl who enjoyed drama and I were children; we were out of school for the summer. My uncle Karl was teasing her and calling her fat, and then he called her slop. She told him to stop calling her that, but he proceeded to call her slop again. Don't you know, that girl went home and lied to her brother? She told him that my uncle had slapped her! He never did that. Her brother fought my uncle because of a damn lie! She was as bad as white women who claimed a Black man had talked to them, back when talking to a white woman wasn't permitted. Then I thought about our last phone call, which went like this:

"I wanted to let you know that I don't appreciate the time that you went and said what you said to my son's father," she said. (She must've had a whole conversation in her head before calling me.)

"What? What are you talking about?" I said.

"I'm talking about the time you went to my child's father's door and said something to him," she answered.

"Oooooh!" I said. "You're talking about the time when you came and picked me up from my house, without me knowing you were coming by, to get me to ride with you to his house? Because I was at home minding my business. That's the time you're referring to? And on the way there, you were telling me what to say to him? Is that the time you're talking about?"

"It sure is," she said with an attitude.

*Okay*, I said to myself. Someone please help me to understand how *according to her*, in their alleged relationship, the dude didn't even want to be with her; how did that, have anything to do with me? Not only that, but *according to her*, the dude didn't even want their child. So, what she was exemplifying was misguided anger. She should've been mad at herself for having a baby with that dude after he had stated his true feelings.

"Well, feel how you feel," I told her. "I was not in the wrong for anything."

She hung up the phone, and that was the last time I spoke with her. And now here she was calling like that conversation never happened! Of course, I ignored her calling me from an app.

My sister's favorite color was pink, so I asked all of the women to wear a shade of pink to the funeral to honor her. My brother said, "The men aren't too proud to wear pink. We are riding hard for my sister." The day of the funeral, Erika—the same woman who had played the violin during Audrey's services—came to show her respect. I was so blessed by her presence. She doesn't realize how much it meant to me for her to be there. I thank Erika, because she's an awesome prayer warrior, and I remember my auntie Geneva telling me once, "A good friend is a praying friend."

***

I'd been going to the gym five days a week, and sometimes I'd go to two different gyms, just to take the class of an instructor named Mario. His class was *fiyah*! So, I was working out a lot, on the equipment and in class, and I thought I was properly hydrating my body.

On July 22, 2022, I was in the kitchen at the stove making a peanut-butter-and-banana sandwich on whole grain bread. My breathing felt shallow, almost as if someone had their hand over my mouth. Something told me to step back from the stove and lean against the sink and countertop.

Everything went dark.

I don't know how long I was passed out, but eventually I heard my name being called, and it sounded like the person was a long distance away from me. Then I heard my mother's voice: "Please wake up, baby. Wake up for your mama."

When I opened my eyes I asked, "Why did I lay down on the kitchen floor to take a nap?" I still hadn't realized that I'd fainted. My legs were beneath my bottom—you know, in that seated position that only a toddler can do and not be in pain afterward. I felt something on my lip, and thought at first that I'd drooled while "taking a nap." Then I realized it was blood. My left front tooth had gone through my bottom lip.

"Lord, I just lost one daughter," I heard my father say. "Please don't let me lose another one." He came into the kitchen and said, "The 911 operator said to stay on the floor and don't try to get up."

I was trying to work my legs from beneath my body, but they were so stiff. My knees had swollen that quickly. When the firemen arrived, they checked my blood pressure and asked me what the last thing I remembered was. I told them that I had been making a peanut-butter-and-banana sandwich.

"Your pressure is 92 over 40," the fireman with the blood pressure cuff told me. "We are going to help you stand, and while you're standing, we will check again, okay?" I nodded and stood, and as he rechecked my blood pressure, I saw the puzzled look on the fireman's face. They walked me to the chair and told me to sit slowly. He told the other fireman that my pressure had dropped while I was standing. Before he could say another word, in came the paramedics. They wanted to know if I had been taking any illegal drugs, and which medications I had been prescribed.

The female paramedic told me that the blood pressure medication I was on was too strong. They were advocating for me to go to the hospital, but… not me! I had to call my doctor's office before the paramedics left, to inform my doctor of the incident. That day, the doctor sent a new prescription to Walgreens for my blood pressure, and told me I needed to go to the hospital. I was not going to the hospital! I was going to Vegas in 11 weeks! They were not about to keep me for an extended stay. Due to my defiance, the doctor had a heart monitor sent to my home, and I had to wear that thing for seven days.

My 50th birthday was 77 days from May 24. My sister knew of my plans to go to Laguna Beach, California, and to Las Vegas—now she told me she was going on the trip with me. I laughed so hard and told her that she wasn't going because she needed to pack a bag and go to the house with our parents.

My birthday trip could have been much better. My travel buddy, Quinetta (my cousin) was with me, and my so-called best friend was with us, too. I had instant regrets for inviting my so-called best friend, because she kept speaking negatively about people—including me. I just recall thinking to myself, *she must lack confidence or something; I mean, confidence isn't thinking you're better than anyone else, it's realizing that you have no reason to compare yourself to anyone else.* I wanted to tell her that judgment is a reflection of character, and what we judge in others reflects what is inside ourselves. She and I exchanged words, and I let her know straight up, I was there to have a good time and enjoy celebrating my birthday, not to argue and be petty.

When my cousin and I were alone, she asked me, "How in the hell do you have someone like that as a friend? Didn't she say she was your best friend?"

"I wouldn't call her my best friend, because we have nothing in common and she always seems so competitive," I told her. "I'm in competition with no one but my damn self!" I felt like a real best friend would know things about me. Like my values, fears, joys, boundaries, triggers, dreams, history, and my heart. She didn't know these things about me. I can say with absolute certainty that she kept an emotional distance, she would change her number without updating me, disappear and move on, then suddenly reappear. To me, that is not best-friend behavior. That is inconsistent-person behavior. She only reappeared when she *felt* like it. Which meant our *friendship* was on her terms, not mutual ones.

She had two moments that change her entire world, and I knew nothing about either one, until she'd had her children. That's not best-friend behavior. That's not even *friend* behavior. That's "*we talk sometimes*" behavior. We met our sophomore year of high school, we were around each other, we shared space, and we *had* history.

While we were in California, I was talking to her about the time that she had gone with me to Bi-Lo to see the girlfriend of the motorcycle man. She told me she didn't remember and said to me, "I only remember the stuff that was important." Basically, she was saying to me, without literally saying to me, that moment wasn't meaningful to me. And that I wasn't meaningful to her in that way.

I thought I had a misunderstanding of what friendship truly was, but it turns out that I was surrounded by people who didn't know how to be friends. I've never had a *friend* to match my loyalty, my efforts, nor my generosity. I definitely did not have a friend that matched my emotional intelligence, my consistency, or my depth. I found myself celebrating folks' birthdays and gifting them, while they didn't bother to get me a 99¢ card for my birthday, from the Dollar Tree.

Perhaps her inability to be a true friend was influenced heavily by her cousin… quick back story. I met this associate in high school… she let me know that she was raised by her aunt who had two children of her own. She and her cousin were close… but I don't know when they decided to start calling one another sisters because in high school, they referred to one another as cousins. Her cousin was maybe three or four years younger than us, so she wasn't actually in high school with us. *BUT* one day as adults, her cousin said to me, "I remember when we lived on Booker, I couldn't stand yo ass!" She laughed, and I laughed along with her, but I made a mental note… I won't be in the company of people who dislike me. *What she hated in me, was the very things that were missing in her… I had no other option, but to keep being fully myself, unapologetically.* So, either my so-called *best friend* didn't know how to be a friend, or she was heavily dependent upon her cousin's perception of me.

People don't "accidentally" reveal dislike. They reveal comfort. When someone feels bold enough to say: "I couldn't stand you." It means they have felt that way for a very long time. And they felt safe enough to finally say it out loud. What she said was not a joke… that was a confession wrapped in humor. But… I caught it. I didn't overreact, I just took note of her sentiments, because that's what emotionally intelligent people do.

My spirit picks up on everything and I am certain that's why I have never had a true best friend, or any friend for that matter. And it wasn't because I am hard to love… but because my spirit is too sharp to tolerate misaligned energy. One thing I am thankful for learning in life is that a lot of times when people have an issue with others, it's because of their own insecurities and inabilities. It really has *nothing* to do with you.

After that trip, I hardly spoke to my so-called best friend. God only knows which version of *her truth* she told other people to make me look like the bad guy… and apparently something spicy was said, because her son unfriended me from a social media platform. But you know what? All of that was okay because, if I gained absolutely nothing by associating myself with her or them, what could I have possibly lost by leaving them all alone.

# New Orleans

Prior to my sister's passing, our cousin Quinetta had come over to introduce me to her best friend. It turns out, I had actually attended the same high school with her friend—but that didn't necessarily create a bond between her friend and me. I was talking on the phone with my sister when they arrived, and after they left, I told my sister, "Something about that visit felt off. Like, I got a really bad vibe."

My sister's voice had so much concern when she asked, "Why would you say some mess like that? Why do you have a bad vibe, Angie? That's Netta, our cousin. So, what? You think they're gonna try to push you off the boat?"

I told her that I couldn't put my finger on it, but something about their presence felt like it had a heavy, negative energy.

They had come by to make their final payment on their portion of a trip we were planning to take together. We were going on a cruise to Montego Bay, Jamaica; Cozumel, Mexico; and Grand Cayman, Cayman Islands. And since the ship would be sailing from the Port of New Orleans, we planned to take a road trip from North Carolina to Louisiana and attend the French Quarter Festival, a music celebration, while we were there. I offered to get my cousin some new outfits for the trip, and even when we were out shopping, I was still picking up on weird energy from her. It was a heavy, dark, and overwhelming feeling. I didn't know what she was up to, so I watched with intent.

After the shopping spree with her, I dropped her off at home and stopped by a different store to see if I could find some crazy socks. While I was in the store, a mother came in with her child; he was probably three or four, maybe five at the most. I heard her tell him that she would have to come back when she got paid to get him the new shoes he needed. Something about the way she said that made me think back to when I was younger, and how it seemed that my sister was always able to get whatever she wanted, while I had to wait.

I walked over to this mother with a smile on my face and said, "Excuse me, ma'am, how are you today?"

She looked at me and smiled back, and said that she was just okay that day.

I said hello to her son and proceeded to tell the mother, "I don't mean to pry in your business, but if you get the shoes that you want for your son, you can meet me at the register and I will pay for them. You can get him some socks, too, if you'd like."

I did not know the lady was going to stand there and cry. Oh, my *gawd*! I told her, "Ma'am, I don't cry pretty, so please, don't make me cry with you."

She began telling me how she was going through a very rough time in life and didn't know that she'd be walking into a blessing. I asked her if she needed shoes, too, and she said, "No, ma'am. Absolutely not. Getting shoes for my baby is enough. Do you mind if I give you a hug?"

I leaned in to hug her, and whispered a prayer. When we got to the register, the cashier was standing there wiping her eyes. She said, "In all the years that I've worked her, I have *never* witnessed anybody do what you just did. God is going to bless you!"

The lady's son ran and gave me a hug, and they went out of the store with his new shoes on his feet and the old shoes in the bag. The cashier waited until they were gone and said, "I wish more people had a heart like yours." I told her I had to ask forgiveness from a lot of people *including myself*, and that I had to heal from past hurts so that I was no longer hurting people intentionally. I told her how I remembered the old clichés about how it was nice to be important, and that it was more important to be nice. Truth is, there's a difference in being kind and nice… thankfully, I've changed, and now I am both. Being kind is rooted in my character — it's who I am when no one is watching. Being nice looks like warmth without an agenda, friendliness that doesn't shift depending on who's watching, and courtesy that isn't tied to getting anything back. I thank the good Lord for changing me.

***

April 14, 2023, was the day of the road trip. We left at five thirty in the morning, and before we got on the road, I asked the driver, Netta's friend, if she had a full tank of gas and said if not, we could gas up before we left Charlotte. On the way to the gas station—I don't know exactly how long we had been on the road—my cousin tried to start an argument, but I kept taking the high road. I knew that my earlier intuition was not wrong. I'd never seen her act like this toward me. When we stopped at Pilot for gas, the driver said she was going to go in to pay for the gas, and I told her no she was not! That was my responsibility. There was an Arby's inside the Pilot, and I offered to pay for their food. For one, I knew my cousin did not have a lot of money; I also didn't know what her friend's pockets were looking like. Besides, if I'm eating out, I'm not going to eat while everyone else has nothing.

We finally made it to New Orleans, and what I can tell you with absolute certainty is this: I will never again ride in a car for that long! Ain't no way. My back and knees were aching like nobody's business! Needless to say, the drawbridges were beyond frightening. After we got checked in to the hotel, I asked the driver twice if she would mind taking me to Walgreens to get some Tylenol after she was rested. She lay on the bed like she didn't hear a word I said.

So, I called for Quinetta, and when she came into the bedroom, I asked her how she ordered groceries when she was at home. She told me it was through an app called DoorDash, or Instacart, or sometimes from Amazon. I asked her if she would place an order for some things, and I would give her the cash for it, because I had never used Door-Dash or Instacart at that point. She said she would order it, and when she told me the fees, I didn't care because I was in pain. When her friend saw that my cousin was about to help me, then and only then did she speak up and say she'd take me to the store to get Tylenol.

We ended up going to a Walmart Marketside, where they sold only groceries. My cousin heard me telling a guy that he was holding up traffic, and damn if her thirsty ass didn't stop in her tracks from the other aisle to jump in the convo! Not that I was trying to holler at him, but damn. She'd done that to me before in the past, but I'd never sweated it, because if a dude was really interested in me, he would've moved right past her. She ended up getting his number, and they chatted on the phone for a bit that night.

The following day, I suggested we go to the French Quarter Festival, and in all honesty, the driver never seemed to like any ideas that I pitched. When my cousin asked me what the festival was about, I told her that I had never been but Google should have details about it. When she saw the goings-on that Google had captured, she said, "Hell, yeah! I wanna go!"

Again, I could feel the unspoken tension from her friend and thought how my instincts had been spot-on.

By the time we got to the festival, it had started to drizzle. Then the sky became so dark, and the rain began to pour down. We went back to the hotel, and I decided to take a shower and get comfortable. My cousin's friend left the room abruptly, like she was upset about something. Then, about two minutes later, my cousin jumped up, saying, "Where did she go?" Which was a rhetorical question, because she couldn't have expected me to answer that. The truth is, they went back out for my cousin to go meet with the dude from Walmart. Like that was a big secret to keep. I was still tracking, and my BS meter was on high alert! I only learned that they had gone to Walmart because I heard my cousin on the phone with that dude, and he asked her, "Why did you call me if you ain't have nothing to say?" I pretended to be asleep and didn't say a word.

On our way to the Port of New Orleans, I asked the driver if she could stop by Shoe Carnival so that I could purchase some sandals. The only reason she stopped is because my cousin said she forgot her socks and could buy some there. After leaving the shoe store, they stopped at KFC to get something to eat; I went inside to use their restroom, and when I came out, I asked my cousin, "Why spend money on food when you can get food on the ship?"

Then her friend started talking about me eating Flamin' Hot Fries. I was thinking to myself like, *Bitch, worry about your damn own yuck-ass mouth!* I went back to the car and let them do their thing. I do not like KFC; it's too salty and greasy. They got sick from eating KFC and demolished the restroom at the port!

We got on the ship, but my luggage still had not been placed outside my cabin's door, and I needed to charge my phone. They decided they were not going to wait for me to charge my phone, and left their cabin. I asked them, "Are we doing separate activities?" Apparently, that was the plan, because neither of them answered, so I rolled with it.

I thank God in heaven every single day for providing me with a sense of awareness! Day two of the cruise, they dipped again. I was not about to be a hermit on my trip! I went to the comedy shows, the casino, the art shows, and other events that were hosted onboard. Some guy kept trying to get my attention, but I acted like I didn't see him and kept it moving.

Day three, I knocked on their door—we had connected cabins, so I didn't have to go out of my cabin to knock. I talked to my cousin, and I let her know that in that short amount of time, she'd taught me to cruise alone. They had excluded me three different times, and her only defense was, "Don't take it like that." How is one supposed to take exclusion? Mind you, I didn't see her nor her friend again that day.

Day four, we reached Montego Bay, Jamaica. I sent them a message in the Messenger app telling them, "If I don't say good morning to y'all, y'all won't say peep to my black ass. LOL." Although "LOL" was just me softening what I really felt. I kept the chat to a minimum and didn't say anything else after that. Montego Bay was so beautiful. I didn't know where they were when I got off the ship, and they had already shown me that they didn't care what I did, so I went to the bus that transported visitors through the city. I took so many pictures, but I was also very drunk and accidentally deleted every picture and video I had captured up to that moment. I did not wait for my cousin and her friend when I got off the bus, because they had already shown me that this trip was about them. Cool.

Day five, we were in Grand Cayman, Cayman Islands. I was not getting off the ship that day, and surprisingly I got a knock on the inner door, with my cousin asking if I was going out to do any activities. I said no because my knees were aching still, from that long car ride. I don't know if they got off the ship or not, but they had already shown me what my place was, and I intended to stay in it! After taking my shower and getting dressed, I went to the deli and got a chicken BLT with Swiss cheese, and it was bussin! I also got two pieces of thinly sliced Key Lime pie and some cookies. I sat in my cabin for a while and reflected on what had transpired. I couldn't believe that my cousin— my mother's sister's daughter—had shown me a side of her that I never knew existed.

Later that day, I got a knock at my door, and it was my cousin. She'd brought me a salad and some cookies; I guess chastisement had caught up with her spirit. I thanked her for bringing me something, and didn't tell her I had already eaten. When I saw my porter, I gave him the plate of food and cookies. The whole time, I was thinking, *Y'all have been acting shady towards me; I don't know if you had ill intentions when you got the food.* I took a nap, and when I awakened, I took another shower, got dressed, and went to the other comedy show. It was hilarious!

Day six, we were in Cozumel, Mexico. Something I said to my cousin must've registered in her mind, because they were actually waiting for me to exit the ship. Their posed presence felt so weird, because the damage had already been done, and it was too late to "play nice." When I returned to my cabin, I showered. That sun was not anything to play with! I was sweaty, and I hate being sweaty. I waited until I no longer heard them, then I went to get a burger. Because who doesn't go to Guy's Burger Joint while onboard? I went back to my cabin to brush my teeth and freshen up, then I went right back out the door to the comedy show. I love to laugh.

Day seven was a fun day at sea. In spite of what had happened, I was still enjoying myself on my cruise. I went to lunch after I'd bathed and gotten dressed. I sat eating solo, minding my business, and then they popped up. I quit eating my food and said I was full, and told them to enjoy their meal.

Day eight, the ship was back in New Orleans. Sooooo… tell me why it really felt like they were trying to leave me there? It would have been okay—I mean, I had my American Express, so I could have easily booked a flight home. I kept calling my cousin's phone, and she wouldn't answer. I saw them in the hallway, then her friend said, "I think I left something in the room. Come and go with me to get it." I went ahead and got off the ship without them. We ran into each other in the parking garage—I was walking in the direction of the driver's vehicle, because I remembered that we had parked in space number seven. She says, "I think we're going the wrong way. My car is back the other way." I kept walking, because I knew she was fucking lying! My cousin was walking along with me.

I could feel that they were up to something, but I never really put my finger on it completely. On our way back to Charlotte, we stopped in Alabama to get gas. So, I got out of the car and said, "If y'all decide to leave, put my suitcase on the sidewalk and I'll take a flight home." They started laughing and I said, "A-hee-hee hell! I'm serious." I purchased a vape pen in the store, and it smelled just like weed. Netta wanted her bestie to turn around and go back to the store so that she could get one, too.

On Sunday, April 23, I was so happy to be back home and away from bad intentions.

The next day at 9:44 a.m., I received a text message from Quinetta saying, "Morning have a wonderful day love you !!"

At 11:05, I reacted to her text with the shocked-face emoji, then I replied:

I am really & truly VERY surprised that you would even be reaching out to me, to say good morning. Considering you didn't know me at all last week! I must admit, though, I appreciate you showing me who you truly are because I never in a million years would've thought I could not trust you. You showed me a side of you that I never knew existed. And please save your apologies because you took every action you intended to take. So, please save your energy. You do not need to apologize for everything you meant to do. I sincerely thank you for teaching me that I am capable of cruising alone!! Your actions proved to me that you really do not rock with me the way that I thought you did. Please keep the same energy you had while on the cruise, I do not want you to feel like it's necessary to tell me good morning AND I certainly do not want you telling me that you love me! I wish I would've known how you were before my dumb tail took you on a shopping spree! I promise to God in heaven, you will NEVER have to worry about Angie Ford ever again! You showed me every day last week that in your eyes, blood is NOT thicker than water! I feel like such an idiot for doing everything I have done for you, & then for you to show me that you felt like, "Fuck you, Angie!" I do not trust you. I do not know you. I will not allow you to ever do that to me again. Please keep the same energy you had last week with your girlfriend. I really feel like y'all were plotting to leave me in Louisiana. You wouldn't even answer my phone calls & want to turn around and say you love me? Y'all made me think about Shanquella Robinson a lot & I said Netta has no idea how jacked up her life is going to be for doing any of what she has done. That is by no means a threat, but you are a Christian, so you already know that God does not like ugly. Please believe me, you do not need to text me good morning & you definitely do not need to lie and say you love me. All I can do is continue praying for you. I wish you the best in life, Netta.

After the book I wrote, her response was, "I apologize for bothering you."

# If Loving Food Is Wrong

For as long as I can remember, people have been saying mean things to me about my weight. Even though I was a young child, my feelings were still capable of being hurt; after all, I am human.

Nicknames that I'm sure were intended to be loving still hurt my feelings. My mother's father used to call me Fat Mama. My mother's brother and his wife used to call me Miss Piggy. My siblings called me Pig or Piggy Wiggy.

Kids in elementary school weren't the nicest, so at that tender age, I managed to block out what they said to me.

The one thing I never got over, though, was a time when I was over at the home of one of my father's sisters one weekend, and one of their other sisters came to pick us up.

Once we were in her car, we saw a Volkswagen Rabbit, and I said, "Oooooh! I want a Rabbit when I get older."

My cousin said to me, "For what? You ain't gone be able to fit in it."

I already didn't feel welcomed in their household, so that incident was even more crushing for me.

Neither one of my father's sisters corrected my cousin. Again, my feelings were hurt, so I just stayed quiet.

The need to belong was loud in my head, and I wanted to be accepted for who I was. It wasn't like I was a 300-pound child—I mean, I was a little league cheerleader for PAL around the age of nine or ten. I even remember the girl who enjoyed drama saying to me that she wasn't spoiled, and that fat kids were spoiled. She was trying to throw shade while standing in the same category she was trying to weaponize. Like, *quit playing with me!* You can't throw a boomerang insult when the boomerang is your exact silhouette.

To this very day, I get so bashful when people tell me I'm beautiful. I guess that's because of the nicknames I had as a child. Plus, I wasn't always beautiful on the inside—I had to fake being nice until I was able to make being nice a real part of my life.

By the time I was 12 years old, I weighed 145 pounds.

Twelve was a tough age.

It was the year I started my period, the year my mother was hospitalized with a ruptured aneurysm—the same thing that had killed her mother—and the year food became scarce in our home.

Before she got sick, my mom cooked every meal. After her sudden hospitalization, I had to learn to cook or go hungry.

The first time I ever made gravy, my father said to our next-door neighbor, "I don't know who in the hell made that white-ass gravy." At that point, it wasn't just about the food—it was about humiliation, dismissal, and being mocked in front of others.

The neighbor responded, "Well, Clyde, at least she's trying. She did the best she could."

I could already tell that he was on some BS by the tone in his voice.

I was minding my business, on the phone with a friend whose nickname was Archie, and my father yelled at me, "Who in the hell are you on the phone talking to?"

"Archie," I said.

Without saying a word, he turned away from me, walked inside the pantry, and returned with a stick—I guess he was planning on beating me with it.

"Archie is a girl," I told him. "Would you like to talk to her?"

"Getcho ass off that goddamn phone," his evil ass said to me.

My sister had already run away from home to live with her boyfriend.

My brothers were out doing whatever boys do.

Being that my father was unfaithful to my mother, a lot of times he'd be absent with his side chick.

With everyone away, where did that leave me?

Alone.

Longing for togetherness with my family.

I had money saved up from birthdays and Christmases, so I'd walk uptown to McDonald's or Burger King to get something to eat. I'd always make it back home before my father returned. One thing about me, I was gonna eat!

On the way back from whichever fastfood spot I chose, I'd stop by Paso's for a pack of Now and Later candy and a bag of bacon-flavored crunchy Cheetos.

By the time I was a sophomore in high school, I weighed 220 pounds.

For a female, I'm considered tall—five foot seven and three-quarters (I just say I'm five foot eight).

I wasn't a sloppy 220.

I was solid.

And… maybe… just maybe… it didn't help that Hog Heaven and Steak N' Hoagie were within walking distance of our house. So, guess where I was! Especially since my father wouldn't allow me in the kitchen after he and my mother went to bed.

Throughout high school, I tried the Slim Safe Bahamian Diet by Dick Gregory. It was a meal-replacement system.

Listen!

That stuff was pure chalk, no matter how I blended it! Orange juice should have never been a suggestion, water was out of the question, and milk was just wrong!

And during this era, I also tried SlimFast. Of course, this was the '90s, when you had to mix the powder with water or milk.

See how those "loving nicknames" had me on a quest that I probably shouldn't have been on? But I had been exposed to body shaming.

After high school, I kept seeing commercials and news reports about Medifast. I believed the hype because the ads had doctors in lab coats (actors), and "clinically proven" was stamped on everything.

Out of pure desperation, I called the advertised number, made an appointment with the clinician, and shelled out hundreds of dollars for packets of powder that tasted like chalk and hope.

In the commercials, they made it sound like I would be joining some elite, scientific program, when really, it was just very expensive powdered shakes and a strict calorie plan.

I didn't know how to get healthy because it was never a topic in my household. We ate what our mother cooked, and most nights she made biscuits or cornbread from scratch to accompany whichever meat and vegetables she prepared. We weren't seated at a table with options, and that was the end of the story.

OMG! Don't let her cook some liver sauteed in onions and simmered in gravy.

I shan't!

I refuse.

I remember her saying to me, "You'll eat it before it eats you." I had planned to let the liver stay on my plate, but she went upstairs to use the bathroom, and my sister told me she'd eat my liver if I ate her sweet peas.

Bet! Done.

To this very day, I will not eat liver. Chitlins either.

Revoke my Black card. I am not eating intestines. As much as I hate oatmeal, if I had to choose between oatmeal and chitlins, I'd pick oatmeal.

I met my six-foot teddy bear while I was on Medifast. I fell in love and said, *To hell with a liquid diet!* In no time, I was back up to 220 pounds.

I remained 220 until I had sarcoidosis and began losing weight rapidly. This was a scary time in my life, because the different specialists I'd gone to couldn't tell me what was wrong.

Then I went to Dr. Iris Cheng. She gave me my diagnosis and prescriptions.

I had to rub an ointment on the raised marks on my skin—it really looked like I had ringworm that was on steroids! The rings looked angry on my skin, as the doctor described it.

I had to be placed on a steroid for my lungs to get clear, and pain medicine for the joint pain.

I got down to 180 pounds, but the weight loss was not on purpose. I could only eat a child-size burger, no French fries or dessert. And sometimes, I would be full after eating half of the burger.

Once my skin healed from the raised rings caused by sarcoidosis, I briefly reconnected with Mr. Motorcycle Man, and after our flame went out forever, my weight returned to 220 pounds.

Once I moved to Sanford, Florida, and became acclimated there, my eating changed drastically. I found myself eating how I wanted to, because my father was not there telling me what I could and couldn't do.

I was in my own place, and that meant I could make a banana pudding and eat it from the bowl if I wanted to. I didn't have to worry about hearing that it was too hot to have the oven on, "Don't be in my kitchen cooking," and "Turn the damn stove off."

I could turn my oven on!

Every week, I found myself baking peanut butter cookies, and that went on until I was sick of eating them.

I spiraled.

I believe that living in Florida was a liberating stage for me, because I was able to eat my ice cream and not be judged!

Food had gotten so good to me that I made up a parody of Luther Ingram's song "If Loving You Is Wrong, I Don't Want to Be Right." I had a pack of chicken drumsticks that I was rinsing, the canola oil was slowly heating, the seasoned flour was waiting for the clean chicken, and I began to sing, "If loving food is wrong, I don't wanna be right. If being right means being without you, I'd rather have some shrimp fried rice."

Oh, hunni, I was grown—grown when I prepared my first meal after six in the evening! No one to tell me that it was too late to be cooking, except the doctor, who seemed to rain on my food parade.

In 2005, when I went to my OB/GYN for my annual lady exam, she did an A1C check and let me know that I was borderline diabetic. I was thinking to myself, *Ms. Doctor Lady Ma'am, mind your damn business! I'm here for my annual Pap, and you're over here trying to be my primary care physician.*

During my visit, when she did the Pap smear, she stuck her finger up my rectum.

*Bitch!*

I almost lost it in that office. How dare she violate me? She didn't even invite me to dinner or a movie!

I was so angry after that appointment, I called my mother, and I could hear Mrs. Jackson laughing in the background. Mama had me on speakerphone, and I'm not made for speakerphones. My filter doesn't work sometimes.

I hadn't known what it meant to be borderline diabetic prior to stepping into that doctor's office.

I knew that it was time to get serious about my health. I had gained weight because I was still on Prednisone due to the sarcoidosis, and had the liberty to eat what I wanted. At this point, I didn't know my exact weight, because my bathroom scale did not go beyond 300 pounds. One of my coworkers had suggested something called the blood type diet. I just looked at her like I was truly engaged in what she was saying, but the whole time I was saying to myself, *This is not backed by science.*

One day, I heard on the news, "The latest in weight loss. Is it the new fad? More coming up after the break." Well, they had my undivided attention, until they came back and went to a different story, which made me forget why I was watching the news in the first place.

Maybe a week or so later, a different news station was covering "the new diet craze that's sweeping Florida." I was not going to miss the story this time, so I stood in front of the television and learned about the South Beach Diet. I turned on my computer and ordered a copy of the book from Amazon.

The diet consisted of salads and the elimination of certain foods followed by a slow reintroduction. I also failed at this diet. It was expensive. I couldn't afford it at the time, so I regained weight.

In 2010, when I moved back to North Carolina, I weighed 338 pounds!

I joined the YMCA, took swimming lessons, did Zumba, and remained faithful to a low-carb, high-fat diet. I enjoyed having things like loaded cauliflower, because I could doctor it up to taste like macaroni and cheese.

No lie.

I also learned how to make THC edibles, and that was the end of the low-carb diet!

In 2020, COVID came and shook up our community. We were sent home to work, which was fine, but I began stress eating. Unnecessary eating. When I got on the scale and saw 327 pounds, I was disappointed with myself.

I restarted the low-carb, high-fat diet, and by the time we returned to the office twice a week in 2023, I was down to 242 pounds. This time, I was going to the gym. I had signed up to use the fitness plan offered through the benefits on my job. I started working out with a personal trainer—a nice lil tender, but I'm no cougar.

Somewhere in this time span, the florist with the Aquafina-size anatomy reached out to me via text. We texted for a bit back and forth, and he congratulated me on my weight loss. Then, true to his character, he started trying to ease into sexting.

I replied to his text, "I have a question I'd like to ask you. I feel like we may have touched on the subject before, but I'm not 100% certain that we did."

"I'm good," he wrote back.

I took that to mean go ahead with my question, so I proceeded to ask him, "Do you know Jesus? Just curious, because everyone has a belief in a higher power, whatever that power is to them. I'm just curious, though."

His reply showed pure agitation: "Sorry to answer your question with a question but does anyone really know Jesus?"

I giggled. "I'll take that as a no. Thank you 😊"

"That's a real question u didn't ask what I believed in u said do I know Jesus I ask a real question does anybody really but religion is one of them things u cant ask questions so I dont partake personally its too decisive," he retorted.

As if I hadn't ruffled his feathers enough already, I hit him with, "A person who knows Jesus would've responded differently. Religion is different from Jesus. It's two different things."

He hit back with some sass! "Well I guess dont and im not ashamed of that because I guess its a frame of mind that somebody personally has to be a part I've never made it there I think to literally."

Not leaving well enough alone, I said, "*Religion* is a range of social-cultural systems, including designated behaviors and practices, morals, beliefs, worldviews, texts, sanctified places, prophecies, ethics, or organizations, that generally relate humanity to supernatural, transcendental, and spiritual elements, although there is no scholarly consensus over what precisely constitutes a religion. I didn't ask with an intent to be offensive. I asked because I'm curious."

I allowed him to have the last word: "I wasn't offended."

I haven't heard from him since.

I told myself that I'd won. What I did was give him a little strategic sanctification. I didn't just shut him down—I shut him *out* with a question so spiritually loaded; it doubled as a block button.

That wasn't shade. That was a *divine exit strategy*.

I knew exactly what I was doing. I didn't cuss him out. I didn't entertain the sexting. I didn't even waste energy on a dramatic goodbye.

I dropped one question—"Do you know Jesus?"—and watched him spiritually ghost himself.

And do you know the best part? I didn't even have to block him. Jesus did it for me.

Ugh! Then I got out of hand again, because the scale read 317 pounds.

I got back on the low-carb, high-fat diet and did well until I was sure I had the hang of things. I kept getting stalled in my weight loss, and that was so frustrating.

Yo-yo.

Gave up again.

Now, in 2026, my health care provider has me on a GLP-1. So far, so good. I was afraid of starting these injections, because I'd heard so much about people being nauseous and I wanted to avoid that feeling as much as possible. I spoke candidly with my health care provider about it, who told me that the people who typically experience the nausea and vomiting generally have not altered their eating habits. They don't change their portion sizes, and they keep consuming greasy foods. Mental note taken. That was not going to be me. I began the injections on December 1, 2025, weighing 302 pounds, and as of January 2, 2026, I weighed 284 pounds.

I believe I will be successful this time. Especially since I've found a sweet treat that literally tastes like cheesecake to me!

I have a provider who listens and genuinely cares. The fact that he told me he was proud of me, and encouraged me to continue doing well on my journey, made a big difference. It's sad that the world of science didn't name obesity as a disease until 2013. I had contemplated weight-loss surgery several times when I lived in Florida, but thank God, I didn't do it. That is a lifetime alteration.

# I Found Me

I starting writing this memoir on Friday, December 26, 2025. around eleven thirty p.m. By Monday, January 12, 2026, I'd written 15 full chapters. Initially my goal was to write 15 chapters. Doubt would begin to set in, but then my mind would give me spurts of memory, and I would continue writing. I set a goal and exceeded it. By ten o'clock on January 19, I'd completed the 18th chapter. I didn't know I had so much to share. But my prayer is that the words I've shared will reach people and help them to begin their healing process. If you were assaulted, regardless of what anyone says, it was not your fault. Hold your head up, adjust your crown, look in your mirror and say, "I love you" to the face looking back at you.

Most times, I was awake until four o'clock in the morning writing.

I'd make myself go to sleep but then be right back up at eight o'clock, to tend to my parents and resume writing.

Admission: I slowed down to almost a halt while writing the chapters titled "The Layoff" and "Still A Caregiver" because the things that happened to me in those chapters will identify the persons involved, even without my mentioning their names. I think I was concerned with exposure, but I said to myself, "They should have been better to me! They caused me mental harm, and therefore, it is my story to tell!"

When I gave myself permission to be okay with that exposure, it felt like I'd ignited something inside of me! I told myself that this had to be the moment every memoirist hit when the fear of exposure finally bows to the truth of the story.

And what I just articulated was one of the most powerful emotional thresholds in writing:

*"They should have been better to me."*
*"They caused me mental harm."*
*"It is my story to tell."*
That's not revenge. That's reclamation.

I allowed myself to be perfectly clear with myself, and I told myself that I was not outing anyone. I was not naming names. I was not fabricating harm. I was, however, simply refusing to protect people who had not protected me.

And that shift—that internal permission—was exactly why my writing suddenly felt sharper, freer, more honest. I was no longer tiptoeing around the truth. I was walking straight into it with my head up.

Here's the deeper thing that was happening: I stopped prioritizing their comfort over my healing.

For years, I carried the emotional weight of what they had done. I carried the silence.

I carried the shame that wasn't mine. I carried the fear of how *they* might feel if *I* told the truth.

But the moment I said, "They should have been better to me," I shifted the moral responsibility back where it belongs.

I reclaimed my narrative power.

My memoir isn't about exposing people. It's about exposing truth.

And truth has consequences. Not because I am malicious, but because they were careless.

I am *not* writing to punish. I am writing to *understand, heal,* and *document.*

The people who harmed me mentally had already written their part of the story through their actions. I am simply writing *my part.* And my part is the one that matters now. I am not being reckless. I am being honest. I am being brave. I am being free.

This process taught me that God made it possible for me to attend college. He needed me to learn how to write academically, so that I could write professionally.

# The Layoff

I had to be on repeat, telling myself to be careful what I asked the Lord for. I am reflecting back to 2008 for a moment, and will build up to present day. That was the year that I quit using relaxers, cut my hair, and went natural. I had the whole audacity to pray and ask the Lord for patience. I was starting to feel an emptiness, and I think that was because the man from California was familiar and I wasn't open to meeting anyone new. But I needed to move past him, too. I kept praying for patience. Then, one day, *bam!* When I tell you there were several storms raging in my life. Baby! And… as if that weren't enough, when I least expected it, here God came with something new I had to learn. What I also understood was, in that season, sometimes God intentionally put me in places *alone*, because He needed me to realize I did not need anyone but Him!

I was fired from both of the last two jobs I held in Florida.

It is such an ugly truth, but the truth no less.

In 2008, I was working as a human resources assistant at a company called Hubbard Construction. I loathed that job! Everyone in the office wanted me to screen their calls, and I was not feeling any of that. It seemed that they'd have me do any task they didn't want to complete. I had to sort the files that everyone in the office kept getting out of order. Like, how do you not know that "S" comes before "Z" or that "Ch" is its own category? I even set it up in a way that the files were alphanumeric, to try to make it easier for them.

They were used to being disorganized.

The drive to work was not short. I lived in Sanford, FL, which was about 30 minutes from Orlando… and the company was in Winter

Park on Lee Road, about 10 minutes east of Orlando.

Every morning on my way to work, I would see a man who appeared to be homeless, and I would say to myself, *Things could be worse.* I could have been in his situation, and Lord knows the streets are not for me! One day, I decided to take my last $20 bill and go buy some deli meats, a loaf of bread, mayo, and chips. I didn't have another dime to my name and was struggling to feed myself, but it was tearing at my heart that the man might be hungry or disoriented. I didn't know what his situation was, but I prayed about it and decided to fix him as many sandwiches as a loaf of bread would make.

I took some drink mix packets and added them to some bottles of water. Put some chips in some Ziploc baggies and put his sandwiches in the other baggies.

The following morning, I went the same route as I'd always gone.

I didn't see the man lying on the bench.

I decided to drive slowly down Lee Road, hoping to see him. Just then, I identified him by the soiled overcoat he wore. I pulled over out of traffic, and as he approached my car, I got his attention. I asked him if I could pray with him… he didn't respond, but I prayed anyway. I handed him the bag of groceries, and told him to have a nice day.

Something about giving to someone in need satisfied my heart.

When I got to work, I was in very good spirits after helping someone less fortunate. I didn't realize that annual reviews were being completed that day, and I figured maybe they'd pay me more than the crap they'd offered when I was hired. Not only was the pay deplorable to begin with, but the raise I got after my review was just as hideous.

"Wow!" I said. "I cannot begin to imagine what I can do with 20 whole cents!"

My cynicism pissed the office manager off, but I didn't care that I mocked the raise. And my smart mouth was the real reason for my termination. She tried to make it seem as though I was fired for wearing a sweatshirt with jeans and sneakers on *casual* Friday! My clothes were clean. There were no holes in my clothing or shoes. My hair wasn't frazzled, and I was in alignment with what everyone else had on. As a matter of fact, the office manager had on a sweatshirt with a damn suit jacket! TF?

She called me into the assistant manager's office and said to me with a grin on her face, "Chris and I were talking, and we have decided to make today your last day with the company. I mean, look at you. Look at how you're dressed. Do you have anything you'd like to say?"

"Thank you for the opportunity to work here," I said. "Have a pleasant day!"

I got my belongings, went home, and applied for unemployment benefits while waiting to hear back from some companies I'd applied to. Unemployment benefits in Florida were a joke! Regardless of how much you earned on your job, the maximum amount you could collect was $275 each week. And the checks were distributed biweekly! During my interview with the unemployment agent, he asked me what sort of business Hubbard was, and I told him it was construction.

"That is ludicrous!" he told me. "I could see if you had to wear a suit and heels every day, my gosh! It was a casual Friday. Don't worry, Ms. Ford, I am approving your unemployment claim."

That happened in January.

By March, I was working as a consumer resolutions specialist for a telecommunications company in Altamonte Springs; it was a closer commute to my apartment, than Winter Park. Not an upgrade, but a job to pay the bills and keep my head afloat. I was not a good customer service representative, because when customers gave attitude, I gave it back.

One day, my supervisor heard me giving attitude and reported me to his boss. I was called into her office with both of them, and she asked me if I'd told a customer what the supervisor had presented to her. Why lie? *You have the recording of the call. So, do what you're going to do.*

"Yes," I told her. "That is my voice on the recording. Initially, I was polite with the customer, and things went sideways when they called me out of my name."

I didn't care what my supervisor's boss had to say after my confession. Hell, she heard the call, so why would she ask me if I said it? That pissed me off.

She told me that I would be on probation, and if I were to have another incident, it would be my immediate termination.

I did not care! My supervisor had already signed off on my tuition reimbursement, so when I was terminated for the previous incident, I still got the four grand plus my regular paycheck. I didn't like that job and didn't care that I'd lost it!

When the supervisor who fired me saw me later one day at Walmart, his palm-colored ass spoke to me. I guess he was with his wife and children.

"Oh! Hi, Angela!" he cheerfully spoke.

His bleached blonde hair was unmistakable. I cut my eyes at him, and in a slow, steady voice, I said, "Fuck you, Paul!"

Why was he even speaking to me like we'd ended on good terms? Like, he legit had just fired me and had the audacity to speak to me as if nothing had happened? Granted, I was not a good customer service agent, but don't play in my damn face speaking to me!

He couldn't reverse the tuition reimbursement, so he filed a false report with the credit bureaus, claiming that I'd defaulted on my account. I called all three bureaus and let them know that someone must've used my information because I had never lived in an area where Embarq provided services. I let the representative know that I had always had Brighthouse Networks for internet and cable, and could prove it with my monthly statements.

That issue was resolved immediately.

And I still say, *F U Paul!*

When 2010 came, I'd had enough of life in Florida. I couldn't seem to find a job selling boiled peanuts for a nickel! I began taking inventory, and that's how I knew that my auntie Shirley Jean had not been lying when she told me that the Lord works in mysterious ways. I would have remained in Florida had I landed a decent job that I could actually call a career. God knew that my parents were going to be needing me soon. So, in essence, the Lord would not open up opportunities for me, and I finally surrendered what felt like my freedom, to return to the chaos at my parents' home.

I called my father and told him that I was ready to move back to Charlotte, and he said so loudly, "Don't you play with me!"

"I'm not joking, Dad," I said softly, trying not to cry. My voice was shaky and cracking. "I am really ready to come home." The one time when I truly needed him, he came through for me! I will give him his props. He told me that he had to make a few phone calls, and then he would let me know when he was leaving Charlotte to drive down to Florida to get me.

My father and my uncle Thomas came down and moved my belongings back to Charlotte.

The plan was to reside with my parents until I'd saved up enough money to move out on my own. I was in no mood for toxic people, and one day, I was sick of my father speaking to me sideways like I was a damn chap. His petty ass wanted to argue about the type of hairspray I'd purchased for my mother's Jheri curl.

"You are the *only* one that has an issue with the purchase, and it's not even for your hair!" I told him.

He had been trying to show off for the new home health aide that was tending to my mom, and ended up getting his ass embarrassed! His orneriness was nothing new to me; neither was his need to perform in front of others. I told myself to overlook his habit of picking unnecessary fights because his desire to assert control over me was no longer going to be fulfilled.

Still out of work, I was determined to complete my bachelor's degree. I was too close to quit. I accepted temporary assignments with different staffing agencies, but none of them became a permanent placement.

The time had come for me to complete my internship to fulfill graduation requirements. I was an unpaid intern for a company that provided services to clients who were HIV-positive.

After graduation, I began working as a mental health professional for a different company. I really should have done more research on them, but because I knew the hiring manager, I made the mistake of trusting them. They were doing things that caused the State of South Carolina to impose a moratorium on any new businesses who were looking to provide the same services in the area. The job became stressful because of the commute. I was living in Charlotte, and my first three clients were residents of Spartanburg, SC. I racked up 5,000 miles on my brand-new car the first month that I worked that job! Mind you, I'd driven off the lot with only five miles on her. There was no gas mileage reimbursement, so the math was not making sense for me.

After the moratorium was lifted, I had my decision, and I needed to return to the work force quickly. I accepted a position as a benefits specialist for a company called Lash Group from 2015 to 2016. The big back supervisor, I think her name was Lisa, hated the air I breathed! Why? Who knows! That was between her and God. There was a part of processing benefit cards for senior citizens that had to be completed like an exam. I knew that I was taking the correct actions, but she would go in the system behind me and change what I'd entered. I started taking screenshots to prove I had not taken the actions that she and her coconspirator Kei were lying and saying I'd done. I lost that job, and they claimed that it was because I had given a discount to a senior citizen on a day that I was out of office! How could I complete a transaction while I was on vacation? I was able to provide proof to the unemployment office that I was on vacation and what they'd said were in fact lies.

Pearson Education then hired me as a professional test scorer. That job was beyond boring! Thank God it was seasonal. In complete silence all day, we sat and independently worked to evaluate students' responses to subject-related open-ended questions according to a customer-supplied scoring guide. I did this mind-numbing work for two seasons, and then I couldn't bear the thought of scoring any longer.

My resources were borderline tapped TF out! Being that Pearson did its own hiring without the use of staffing agencies, the supervisors prepared their teams for how to successfully draw unemployment, unless we had other jobs lined up.

Being out of work was all too familiar.

I felt like a failure, because I couldn't even get a job at Burger King or McDonald's. On one of those applications, I put my real work experience, and the manager told me, "I love your personality, but you are overqualified for this job." On the other application, I didn't list any work experience and was told, "I need someone who has the bare-minimum experience. And, I mean, you sound well-spoken, but you don't have any experience."

I was desperate to land a job!

I finally accepted a job as a substitute teacher in Rock Hill, South Carolina. The staffing agency was in Rock Hill, but I could work at any of the nearby districts: Chester, Fort Mill, or Rock Hill. I worked in each one, but the pay was awful! That job taught me that teachers really go through a lot in a day, and they were definitely underpaid! I was probably the only substitute teacher singing Cardi B's "Ring"! Word for word. Sunset Park Elementary School in Rock Hill was my favorite school to sub for, and I loved the children. I could tell that they loved me right back. I helped them to understand how to arrive at solutions for their word problems, and it felt good because I was being the person that I had needed when I was their age.

One morning on my way to Chester to sub, it was dark, raining, and cold outside. I cried. I pleaded with the Lord and asked Him why I had to face so many challenges. What did I need to do differently? I was frustrated. Just as I was about to blow my nose, I saw a large black pickup truck with a Dixie flag across the rear window shift into my lane, and it splashed a large puddle of water on my car. I was hot! I told God that I was tired and if this was all I was to do in life, then go ahead and take me because I was at my wits' end. When I arrived at the school, I sat for a moment and got myself together. I was in a classroom with autistic children. The teacher's aide was out with a broken leg, so I had to be at that school for six weeks. And Chester was not a short distance from my home!

I was angry with God.

God knew what He was doing.

I was going to need the substitute experience for what he had in store for me next.

The lint in my pockets was shameful. I mean, I put the "rok" in "broke"! I would have enough available funds one of my credit cards to be able fill up my gas tank. Now, was it actually enough to cover the transaction? No. Which is why I low-key panicked when the cop pulled into the gas station beside my car. I was determined to do life on my own terms without asking anyone for a dime. I'd pawn my jewelry, and then when I'd get it back, I'd have to pawn it again. I absolutely refused to ask anyone for a dime, because people had the tendency of reminding you, "If it wasn't for me, you wouldn't have…"

The last day of Black History Month in 2019, I interviewed with the hiring agency Robert Half. When I returned to my SUV, I sat there and constructed a thank-you email and sent it to the person who'd taken time out of their day to see me. I thought nothing else of it, because I couldn't really get a good read on the interviewer.

On Monday, March 4, I received a call that changed everything! I got the job!

My start date was April 1, 2019. I swear, I thought it was going to be a cruel April Fool's joke, but it was legit. I was hired as a Recruiting Specialist III, for Walmart. The company was located on Water Ridge Parkway, which was in the business park behind the Jock's and Jill's on Tyvola Road. Our training was held offsite at the local Sheraton. So many things went through my mind about the location, because I couldn't understand how Walmart was conducting training at a hotel.

The supervisors leading the trainings went over the expectations for the next two weeks, and let us know that we'd be covering a lot of material and that we were expected to participate. Well, they were passing the microphone around the room, and everyone had to stand and introduce themselves. I swear there must've been a good hundred people in the training. Everyone was so cordial and telling a little about themselves along with their names.

Well. The microphone finally made its way to my table. I stood and said, "My name is Cardi B."

The entire room erupted in laughter. The supervisors were trying to get it together and ask me what my real name was.

I never lived that moment down, because once we were actually in the corporate office, I'd hear someone calling me "Cardi," or sometimes "Blue," because my sistalocs were a beautiful turquoise blue, and had grown down to my waistline.

We had options for which shift we'd work, and I selected eleven o'clock a.m. until eight o'clock p.m. There were maybe five other people from my team who worked the same shift. I would partner up with them, to help them to navigate two of the systems we'd be using. One of the people I helped, Zoe, was as sweet as she could be, but my Lord, she was nosy! The supervisors had told us that there was always someone watching us, and to act accordingly. Well, after the rough bouts I'd had with finding a job, they didn't have to worry about boo from me!

Work was so slow and the office felt like a waiting room. I'd already read the same knowledge articles so many times I could quote them. Out of pure boredom, I asked my supervisor, Whitney, for more work. She arranged for me to go to a different team to shadow some of them and learn their process. They were placing outbound calls to candidates who'd applied and needed to be moved to the next step in the hiring process. I sat with a lady named Katherine Rebescher. I think I made her nervous because I talked so much and I asked a lot of questions. She was so sweet. The next night, I sat with Destiny Keel. She was the cutest petite person. Sharp as a whip! She was very smart. Sharka was their workflow coordinator, and she was rigid about processes.

About two months into this temporary role, my supervisor began calling on me to do special projects. One day, one of my teammates stood behind me and, like a bully, said, "What makes her so special that she gets to do special projects!" It felt threatening, so I informed my supervisor. She was let go the same day, because other people already had complained about her.

All the teams had to come to the team huddle (a meeting) that was in the section where my team sat. One day, Whitney announced to everyone that they would be having a signup sheet for those who wanted to conduct training for the new hires. Given my work history and the number of terminations I'd faced, I felt I was incapable of performing anything except what I was doing currently.

The day came for the people who'd signed up to go in their meeting. I got an email from my supervisor informing me that I needed to be in that meeting, so after I got clocked in, I went to the room where they were. Immediately when I walked in the door, the male recruiting supervisor failed to whisper when he asked Whitney, "Is she supposed to be in here?"

If looks could kill, his ass would've been dead that day! Whitney gave him a firm yes that sounded like, *How dare you question my authority?*

I hadn't signed up to be one of the trainers, so why was I in their meeting?

"I didn't sign up to do this," I whispered to Whitney.

"I know. You were voluntold," she said, flashing her beautiful smile.

The other supervisor, Quan, heard what Whitney said to me, and then said so everyone could hear, "Ms. Angie, that's what you get for showing leadership capabilities." Everyone laughed, even the male recruiting supervisor.

I'm not exactly sure why the male recruiting supervisor didn't like me, but he made it obvious.

"Perhaps he's jealous of you," someone said to me one day.

I frowned and looked perplexed. "Jealous of what? I'm a woman.

Are you saying he'd rather be a woman?" We both laughed.

"You're really smart," the person told me. "And that's threatening to some people."

I knew my educational history, so to hear someone say that I was smart made me wonder if they were being facetious.

The painful memories of verbal abuse were reemerging. Why had my father said those things to me?

Here I was with bachelor's and master's degrees, feeling unintelligent.

"A jealous spirit will cause people to mistreat the very person who could very well be a blessing to them!" I told the person.

The musty spider monkey was supposed to be sending out emails to all the trainers for the upcoming new hires, but he kept leaving me off the email list. Thankfully, Diontez Venable was on top of things, so he'd forward the emails to me. I quit saying anything to the male recruiting supervisor about the emails, because his actions showed his intentions.

Diontez was a tall, brown-skinned, decent looking young man, and he was my neighbor at work, so for the longest time, whenever we'd speak to each other, it was always, "Good morning, neighbor!" Then he said it reminded him of being in church, and would make up a scripture each day. I started calling him "Pastuh"! Funny thing was, other people started calling him "Pastuh," too.

I had finally reached a point where I no longer had to pawn my jewelry to make ends meet for me. No one knew of my challenges. Just me and the good Lord.

While I had abhorred being a substitute teacher, the role actually positioned me to become one of the trainers. My supervisor saw something in me that I didn't know was there. After work one evening, I sat in my car and cried tears of praise and joy! Up until this point in my work life, I'd felt like people at other jobs treated me like they knew I'd had a grade-point average that was less than one in high school.

But God!

He allowed Whitney to see that I was indeed an asset and not a liability.

On September 4, 2019, when I returned from lunch, some of my teammates asked me if I'd seen the email that was sent out. They wouldn't tell me what it was, just told me to check my email.

I didn't know what to expect, because Walmart had just laid off hundreds of people from the finance department. So, yeah, I was hesitant to look at an email.

It was an offer letter!

I had been offered a permanent position as a Recruiting Specialist III. During the huddle that day, Quan and Whitney let us know that there would be two workflow positions available, and that we would be interviewed as if they had never met us before. I knew that I didn't always interview well, so I was not about to apply for either of the positions.

Diontez found himself having to pair up with one of our coworkers from a different team, named Mitch. I called them Tippens & Zurosky for the obvious reason, they were two intelligent men (Tippens & Zurosky were two local personal injury attorneys). Diontez represented the Black attorney (Tippens), while Mitch was the other attorney. The workflow position had initially been offered to Mitch, but he'd also been offered a different role. When Diontez mentioned this to me I knew that he was upset, and I suddenly felt like I had a little brother that I needed to defend. I was honored that he thought highly enough of me to confide in me. I suggested he speak with Whitney about it. He doubted me initially, but I reminded him of *who* he was and *whose* he was—the son of our most high God!

While he spoke with Whitney, I went to the restroom and prayed. Look at how the Lord moved things around so rapidly! Diontez rightfully became the workflow coordinator. He instantly gained some haters, but I had his back no matter what! I shut shit down when folks were talking about him behind his back, and I let Whitney know what I'd said and done, just in case lies floated back to her. Later that day when we were in our huddle to hear about the promotions, Whitney let it be known that workflow coordinators were to be given the same respect a supervisor would receive.

By the end of 2019, Whitney had given her resignation—our team was not told why, and the whole atmosphere shifted. Supervisors from different teams would come and sit with us. They didn't know our processes, so they called on me and Diontez a lot.

One day, we were called into another huddle, where we were told that some of my team would be under the male recruiting supervisor, while everyone else would be under Quan. I do not know why he loathed me the way that he did, because I had never said or done anything disrespectful toward him.

When COVID hit in 2020, we were told that we would not be working in the office until further notice. We had to complete some clearances prior to taking our laptops home, but ultimately, we got it done.

I hated driving in Charlotte, so working from home was perfect for me.

We had unnecessary Zoom meetings every morning, but I'd join the meeting with my camera off and continue working.

The the male recruiting supervisor had taken me off of all special projects, which was cool. As the cliché goes, "One monkey don't stop no show." And he didn't!

He stressed me out to the point where I thought I was having a heart attack! Turns out, it was an anxiety attack. I had to wear a heart monitor for seven days and write down all of my physical activity. During that time, I was actively going to the gym, so I'm sure that monitor ran hot!

Thankfully, roles changed, and I got a new supervisor, his name was LaShard. I introduced myself and let him know that when Whitney was my supervisor, she'd had me on a lot of projects, and that one of the first things the male recruiting supervisor had done was remove me from them. I also told him what the male recruiting supervisor had said the day that I joined the meeting for trainers. LaShard had decency. He apologized for the fact that I had been mistreated, as one of Walmart's core values was to always have respect for the individual, and the male recruiting supervisor had not honored that.

LaShard was my supervisor long enough for me to be put on some special projects and receive recognition for being a subject matter expert (SME). Then the first male recruiting supervisor was going to be my supervisor again. When I learned of that, I began applying to every job vacancy I saw! I did not want to be under his leadership any longer. Well, wish granted because, we ended up getting a female supervisor. But she emulated the male recruiting supervisor's way of *leadership* which kept tension high.

I learned to pray for them, in spite of the circumstances.

Every morning, I'd say a prayer and read Psalm 23.

I was begging God for a promotion.

Then one day, I could tell something was happening, because all of a sudden, I was getting emails from the supervisors for the roles I'd applied to. Even a supervisor who'd flat-out told me she didn't need anyone else on her team contacted me. I told her I was no longer interested. I knew I had to be close to my blessing, because even LaShard had an opening on his team.

I stood 10 toes down, on my mustard seed faith.

I remembered that a similar situation had occurred with a coworker named Teair, and she had been stuck in that role for six months.

I felt like the new female supervisor was harassing me, and I let her know that I was not applying for any other roles. At that point, I had already applied for 31 positions, and I wasn't about to apply for any others! I told her that I had interviewed very well for the facilitator role, and it was given to a different internal candidate. I told her how funny it was that all of these new requisitions were opening up, but then we found out that none of those roles would ever be available.

The thing is, the role I had applied to was an N28, which was supervisory level, but I didn't actually supervise a team.

They were scrambling like roaches when the lights are suddenly turned on!

I kept a sticky note on my laptop that read, "Hebrews 11:6: without faith, it is impossible to please God."

We had another Zoom huddle where the unpleasant male recruiting supervisor let us know yet again that he was being promoted—he had already told us this! Before the meeting ended, he asked if anyone had any questions or concerns.

"Yes. I do," a woman named Marla said.

He chuckled. "Go head, Marla."

"I would like to congratulate Angie Ford on her promotion to an auditor's role," she said.

He sounded like he had some balls in his mouth when he lied and said he didn't know I had been promoted. Supervisors are the first to find out! Hell, even he was trying to get me to accept a position on his team. I honestly said to myself that this must've been the feeling that slaves had when a fuss was being made over them.

I believe I had three or four interviews before being extended an offer, and my new role would begin in September 2021. I was finally promoted to an N28 role! The Lord certainly prepared a table for me in the presence of my enemies.

I felt liberated.

The first day in my new role, I removed myself from the recruiting Zoom thread, and instantly one of the workflows called me via Zoom. I hit decline before it could ring a second time. Then I got a message from Mariah, who was one of the new workflows, asking me why I had removed myself from the thread.

"I am no longer a part of that team," I told her. "I do not need to receive messages regarding the actions being taken for work distribution. If you have any further questions, please direct them to either of my supervisors, Tara or Abey."

It was disturbing how they all tried to play down my promotion, but they were following the directives of the unpleasant male recruiting supervisor. Sheena was the worst! It was like if he told her to bark like a dog, she'd do it. But baby! I had to conduct myself as a woman with class.

"How did you get your master's degree? Did you have to sell an arm or a leg?" Sheena asked me one day.

"How does anyone get their masters? They study for it," I responded.

The fact that she made that statement let me know that they were having conversations about me behind my back.

Even the new female recruiting supervisor became shady. We had started in the same training at the Radisson, and she had made it from a specialist III to a workflow to a supervisor. It didn't mean she'd done anything better than I'd done; it just meant she wanted to be in a leadership role for the wrong reasons.

I was a leader without the title. I didn't need their validation. I was so relieved to be the hell away from them devils! The recruiting supervisors were all under the leadership of a woman whose management style created unnecessary tension.

Because I'd come from a team where I was a SME, I provided a lot of insight into how the team was failing their audits. And in one of our weekly meetings, the musty spider monkey was in his bitter feelings when he said with an attitude, "How come now it's all of a sudden a problem? The team's been passing before. Now there's suddenly a problem."

I didn't open my mouth to say a word. My supervisor, who was in India, spoke up and told the musty spider monkey that there had not been a sudden change. The teams had been given leniency to get their corrections made and start following the knowledge articles.

After the meeting was over, I let my supervisor know that the anger was channeled at me. In India, women are not as outspoken as American women, so the supervisor took what I said with a grain of salt.

I had the opportunity to shadow everyone on the team, which was awesome, because I learned different ways of arriving at the same goal.

During one of our meetings, one of our team members was sharing the highlights from her son's football games, and I said, "Go Big I!" Independence Senior High was "Big I."

"Wait," a woman named Katherine said. "Did someone say, 'Go Big I'?"

"Yes, that was me," I said. "Did you go to Independence?"

Our dialogue took over the meeting.

We spoke offline after the meeting, and you know, it's wild how the Lord allows paths to cross for a reason. We had gone to the same high school and never spoken to one another—she was Katherine King then—she's Kat Rebescher now. Then, decades later, we were in the same corporate setting. I asked her if it was okay for me to call her Kat, because she was too cool for that Katherine business.

"Angie, you are so sweet," she said to me.

"Thugs can't be sweet, Kat," I told her. We had a good laugh afterward.

Here's a prime example of her level of coolness. I texted her, "Check baby check baby one two three four. Check back check baby one two three. Check baby check baby one two. Check baby check baby one."

Kat responded, "All I wanna do is zooma zoom, zoom, zoom, and a boom, boom. Just shake your rump!" She also let me know that she was "off-white, not white." She was so humorous.

My vacation time was always approved instantly, unlike on the team I'd come from—the unpleasant male recruiting supervisor would swear he hadn't seen my request. What does that say about his character?

In 2023, we received a notification that we'd be returning to the office twice a week. COVID had simmered down quite a bit, and it was safe to be within three feet of other people. I still wore my mask, though. We worked back-to-back days in the office; other teams had a weird setup where they'd come in every Monday and Thursday. I was thankful to be on the quality team.

Shortly after our return to the office, a dude with man boobs became our supervisor.

One day in my row, we were sitting and talking amongst ourselves when he came and inserted himself. I don't know if he disliked me or if he disliked life in general, but he looked at me and said, "I remember you had applied for this position, and I said I wasn't going to hire you for it."

Before I could respond, a woman named Toya spoke up: "That's okay. Destiny hired her. She made an excellent choice. Welcome to the team, Angie!"

I finally felt like I belonged. I felt like I was a part of a tribe of people who wanted me to be in their presence. Except for the dude with the man boobs, or as some people call them, "moobs."

Let me help you understand a little better about who LaToya Jackson Reddish is… fashionista does not adequately define her style. On any given day, she'd come into the office with a different wig on—personally, I loved her Chaka Khan wig. She is the only person I knew, who could put together mixed patterns and colors, and still looked like she stepped off the scene of Essence magazine! Toya was so comical, and every day that we were in the office, she kept our row laughing.

The holidays were upon us. It was Black Friday.

I've never been a fan of shopping the day after Thanksgiving, because there are entirely too many people shopping for the same product at the same time! Depending on who you ask, some would say that Black Friday was a day where enslaved people were sold at a discount. I could understand how one would assume that the term "Black Friday" could be tied to racial oppression, but again, this is dependent upon who you ask.

Well, for the first time, in 2023, I participated in Black Friday from the comfort of my home. I went online to see the supposed travel deals that Carnival cruises were offering. Well! I had always wanted to go on a Christmas cruise, and what did I find? A cruise from Miami to Grand Cayman, Cayman Islands, and Montego Bay, Jamaica. It was a five-day cruise that would begin on Monday, December 22, 2025, and end on

Saturday, December 27, 2025. I planned well in advance, just in case I have to pivot. Besides, our plans are not the same as God's plans.

***

On December 27, 2023, I finally packed my luggage for my New Year's cruise.

On December 28, I awakened around two o'clock in the morning. I was too excited to go back to sleep, because it was my first time taking a solo flight. (Quinetta was supposed to come with me, but her circumstances changed.) I am legit afraid of heights, especially in open spaces, but I will get on an airplane. I scheduled a Lyft to pick me up and take me to the airport, and I got on the plane fine.

As I was sitting in my seat, a woman with her toddler on her hip came to my row and loudly said to me, "You are sitting in my seat. You are in the wrong seat. Oh my God! Can't you people read?"

I was absolutely certain that she was talking to herself, so I ignored her initially. Then the flight attendant came over asking for Quinetta. I let the attendant know that she would not be joining me on this trip.

"My name is Angela Ford," I added. "Which seat am I supposed to be in?"

The flight attended pointed to the seat where I was buckled in and said, "You're in the seat you're supposed to be in."

"Oh. Because Karen over here yelled and told me I was in the wrong seat," I told her. "And that I was in her seat." I always book a seat by the window, or the exit door. Karen wanted the window seat, instead of the seat she'd paid for, at the end of my row.

"Is this your toddler?" the flight attendant asked the woman, looking at her.

"Yeah, it is," Karen snapped. "And…?"

The flight attendant didn't miss a beat. "And… this toddler is listed as a lap passenger, which means you'll need to fasten your toddler in your seatbelt with you while they are seated in your lap." Then the attendant looked at me and told me, "I'm sorry for the confusion, ma'am."

As we were exiting the plane, I saw Karen outside the door, tussling with her fussy toddler, and I said loud enough for her to hear me, "Have a happy New Year, and may the Lord bless you."

It didn't matter if she responded or not. What mattered was, I refused to let the devil steal my joy!

After I checked into my suite, I scheduled a Lyft to the Walmart Marketplace and the smoke shop. When I got back in the Lyft, the driver let me know that he was a school resource officer. Mr. Occifer Sir Man! I felt like *Miami Vice* was going to roll up on me at any moment!

On December 30, I took the hotel's free shuttle to the Port of Miami. Police with dogs were everywhere! I sat there like I didn't have anything on me. Technically, I didn't. I had placed my THC vape pen inside my suitcase, and the K-9 must've detected it. I had tipped the bag handler $20 when I handed him my suitcase. I just needed him to separate me from my luggage, and I would be okay. When I went through the first phase of customs, I knew they were onto me, but they couldn't prove it was me. The officer stopped directly in front of me with that huge German shepherd! Talk about a busy bladder. I had to stand unshaken because I did not have anything on me at that point. His K-9 could get my human scent but couldn't trace the THC, because the THC pen wasn't on me. I was smart enough to not have it on me!

I learned in this panicked moment to never do that again. I mean, I'd sneaked ganja on the ships in the past, and this time it was a vape, so I thought it would be undetected. Then I quicky remembered Brittany Griner. I'm glad she was finally allowed to return to her wife and family.

I ended up missing the whole New Year's celebration because I had a strong drink called Kiss on the Lips. I am not a drinker, and that mixed drink proved that!

I woke up on January 1. Happy New Year!

Honduras was beautiful, it was also very hot. The walk from the ship to the beach was decent. I went past an area where sloths were in the trees, but I was not eager to get close enough to see them. There were some cabanas near the shoreline, and I saw a couple outside talking. I asked them if it was cooler inside their cabana, and they told me I could go inside. As soon as I opened the door, I smelled ganja! I exited quickly.

On January 2, we arrived in Cozumel. The land excursion was only $40, and we got to see the residential areas. I probably captured 150 photos. It was so beautiful—the history, the tour guide, the return to the ship. They were all golden. I sped up my pace back to the ship, though, because I'd received an Amex notification that an $80 charge was pending with Carnival. I went directly to the concierge desk. They told me the charges were automatic gratuities. I let the representative know that each day I'd seen Wayman, the porter, I'd given him a $20 tip, and at that point he'd already received $20. I also let her know that anytime I was in the dining room for dinner, I gave a $20 tip as well. She reversed the charge.

On January 4, the day we returned to Miami, I took a few puffs off of my vape pen and left it inside the closet of my cabin. I was not about to deal with customs again. Besides, I wouldn't have been able to get it on an airplane. It had served its purpose. I fell asleep on the flight before we had even lifted off to return to Charlotte.

***

Work went on as usual for the next six months. Then on June 20, 2024, I got an email from my supervisor's boss's boss, Ana. I low-key panicked, because I knew that couldn't be a good thing.

I reached out to everyone on the team to see if they'd received an invitation to a meeting or not. Kat told me to think positive.

"Okay, I am positive I am about to get fired!" I told her.

At 10:44 a.m., Ana began by saying, "Thanks for joining this meeting. I know it was kind of sudden that I scheduled this meeting, but I have some news to share that affects your personal life. We have a value where our current organization is to understand how we can better support our partners and stakeholders. Yet to achieve this goal, we have realigned our business priorities and how we will operate moving forward. It is part of the restructuring that your role has been eliminated. I know this is difficult news to hear and will take time to process, so you will be receiving an email addressed with the full details and next steps by end of day today."

"Okay," I said. "So, as of right now, you are saying I am terminated?"

"Today is your last day with the corporate office," she affirmed. "And your access will be revoked by noon, central time. So, I will share a little bit more about this in a moment. The information we will send you will include details about your benefits, how Walmart can support you during this transition, as well as your severance eligibility. And it is important, so do please read it carefully."

All I could think about was how the hundreds of people had been laid off when I started back in 2019. Ana was still talking, but I had mentally checked out. Did she think I was going to remain clocked in and do any more work when she'd literally just told me I was being laid off?

"I don't know if I missed when you said that I did something personally to cause my termination," I finally said.

"No!" she said quickly. It's not based on performance or anything about what you did or didn't do. It's about business. It's a broader change based on how we want to realign organization to support our needs going forward, and yeah, just this role is no longer needed for the team."

My eyebrows rose. "Oh. Okay. Just my role, no one else's?"

"I can't talk about the scope of this change," she responded. "So we're here to focus on this role. But you will see more information in the email packet, and I encourage you to also reach out to your manager. There will be a phone number to an associate contact center in the email."

I didn't care what she was saying at that point. "I just want to make sure I understand you correctly, okay? So, I've done nothing personally to cause my termination, or layoff, and it's a severance package for my normal pay up until three months, did you say?" I wanted more clarity.

She made a noise like she was trying to clear her sinuses. "So, three months is your nonworking transition, which is where you have an option to look for a new role with Walmart or outside of the company during this time. From now until September 20, you will continue to receive your benefits coverage and your payment on a biweekly cadence as usual. I do have a note about your severance eligibility. I don't have that email open right now, so that would be sent by the team that supports it."

I was still trying not to be numb. Here I was coming up on my fifth anniversary with the company.

"I'm sorry," I said. "It's just that I'm trying to make sure that I fully comprehend what you're saying. Okay. So, it's a severance package where I continue receiving my medical benefits up until September the 20th?"

Yes," she affirmed.

I had a lot of unused vacation time and was paid for that as well.

It bothered me to be let go from a job yet again. It wasn't my fault this time, but that didn't matter, because the feeling was still very familiar.

After my layoff, at least seven or eight other people texted to tell me that they had been laid off, too. It was crazy that Walmart was doing this again. I get that outsourcing jobs saves the company money, but the distrust they created with loyal employees could never be undone. Sadly, everyone who worked at the Water Ridge Parkway office was laid off.

# Still A Caregiver

I felt awful, because I had been under the same roof as my mother day after day and hadn't realized that her health was declining.

I knew that she had diabetes; so, I tried my best to feed her healthier options, like the low-carb, high-fat diet for instance. Trying to get my mom to eat healthier was a whole challenge, because she was so set in her ways.

The year 2024 was giving me pure hell.

In the month of June, I noticed my mother's appetite had drastically changed. It was rare that she would allow food to sit in front of her, and not touch it, so I knew something was seriously wrong. I said to myself in that moment, *God knew that I would need to be here for whatever she is going through right now, that's probably why the layoff didn't make me extremely upset.* I was afforded an opportunity to really observe the changes in Mama's health. She'd gotten to the point where she couldn't stand, even with help. One day, I was helping her in the bathroom, and when she went to stand, she sat back down immediately.

"I can't help it, Angie," she said, looking at me.

Something about the way she said that tugged at my heart. When I got back to my room, I cried out to the Lord, because I knew He knew exactly what was wrong, and only He could prepare me for what was next.

Mama had begun refusing her medications. She had to take several pills for hypertension and some for chronic kidney disease. I placed a call to the after-hours nurse for Mama's health care provider, and I let them know, "My mom is actually showing signs of Alzheimer's and/or dementia. Since the discussion is not being had, allow me to enlighten you of the changes. She's refusing her medications, she won't drink any fluids, and she won't eat."

"Call the medic and have them to transport her to the hospital immediately," the on-call nurse told me.

I called Quinetta and let her know that Mama was on her way to the hospital, and Netta took that to mean, *Show up*. And she did. When she got to the hospital, she called me and informed me, "They are not keeping Mama. She will be released from the hospital in a little bit. But before I get started telling you this, please don't get mad at Mama. And don't tell her that I told you, because I said I wasn't gone say nothing. Mama told me that she is okay and she just wanted to get out of the house."

I didn't question Netta on this, because Mama has done stuff like this in the past, where she sought the wrong type of attention. I thanked her for letting me know what she'd found out, and I kept that one tucked away and just kept a close watch on Mama.

In July, I went to the library to print off the health care power of attorney forms that Mama's doctor's office had sent to me. I figured it would be smart to print one out for my father, too, because his health was declining as well. Upon leaving the library, I went to Mama's doctor's appointment. Neither of my parents knew that I was showing up, but I did because I knew they would not tell the nurse practitioner about the changes that had taken place with Mama.

We spoke about the likelihood of Mama's having dementia or Alzheimer's, and the NP told me, "Being that she's had a stroke, the stroke has a lasting impact on her brain. The side of the brain that controls memory is the side where she had surgery." Then she added, "Your mother will need to be placed on dialysis."

I watched as Mama's head dropped. I knew my mother didn't want to be on dialysis, and as I had power of attorney for her health care, I was going to honor her wishes. She had already started losing muscle mass, because dementia had drastically changed her appetite, and she wouldn't eat. She couldn't feed herself—like, she literally did not have the strength to hold a plastic fork.

"Do you think it's necessary for my mother to still be receiving insulin injections?" I asked the nurse. "She's lost a significant amount of weight, and most days, she doesn't eat."

"We will take her off of insulin immediately," the nurse replied. Then she smiled at my father and gently said, "Mr. Ford, do you understand that? Mrs. Ford is not to receive any more insulin. Do not give her any more shots, okay?"

My mom had an appointment on July 17, and my father drove her across town in triple-digit heat. They got there and was told that her appointment had been canceled. When they got back to the house, he couldn't get her out of their Chevy Equinox. Thankfully, I'd learned from my personal trainer how to safely do dead lifts, because I was able to pick my mother up and put her in her wheelchair. Her breathing was so labored, and she looked like she was going to pass out. As soon as I got her across the threshold, I pressed her Life Alert button, and the firemen arrived before the paramedics did. They had her on oxygen for at least 20 minutes before she became alert.

By the time the ambulance arrived, the firemen were asking her how she was doing.

"I'm fine," she said, "but who are you? And where did you come from?"

I laughed to keep from crying, because I was seeing my mother become someone I did not recognize. Her cognition had changed dramatically. She had lost 40 or 50 pounds in the past seven months!

This time, they kept her at the hospital. She was being treated for dehydration and a lack of oxygen. An agreement was made for my brother to stay at the hospital to relieve my father until I got there. He kept calling my phone talking about getting my mother's dentures. But why did she need them? She wasn't eating anything. I knew she hated the hospital food; plus, her nutrients were coming from an IV. Truth is, he wanted to be anyplace but the hospital.

I arrived at the hospital around two o'clock that afternoon, and the nurse asked which pharmacy our mother used. I said it was the Walgreens on Milton Road. My brother, who thinks he knows every damn thing, wanted to debate me on which Walgreens it was. I mean, had he ever gone to pick up her prescriptions? He decided he wanted to bet me, and I shook his hand on the bet.

"I don't bet unless I know I'm going to win!" I warned him. This was an easy win, because I'd been the person going to get her medicine for her. When my brother saw the proof that he was wrong, he looked like his life had fled his body! I was thinking to myself, *Run me that hundred, though!* The nurse laughed at him and left the room. I already knew that he was not going to pay out on the bet, and didn't expect it. But if *he* had won the bet, he would've been dead serious about collecting his winnings.

July 20, the doctor called and informed me that they'd be releasing my mother from the hospital, and he'd be prescribing a medication to help stimulate her appetite and treat depression. I suppose my mother may have been depressed, considering she'd gone from being an able-bodied woman to being disabled back in the late '80s, and she'd been in a wheelchair ever since that time.

On July 21, my brother came to the house to visit with her. I asked him if he was going to come by to help out, and without him even knowing what I needed help with, he said to me, "You already know I'm not. So I don't know why you're asking."

In fact, if it had been up to my brother, my parents would've been placed in an assisted living facility—he had even suggested it to me. He said, "You've been taking care of Mama nem all your life. It's time for you to have your own life. Let them go to a nursing home."

True, I had been my mother's caregiver since I was 12 years old. It was part of the reason I'd moved to Florida in 2003—I was tired of being the only person to reliably show up when caregiving was needed.

But! This time was different.

When my parents and I went to the notary to sign the health care power of attorney forms, my mother told me, "I don't want to be placed in a nursing home." I was going to do everything in my power to honor her wishes.

One of the ladies I'd met at the gym, Roneca White-Tezino (well, people knew her as Knikki), texted to check on me, because I'd missed going to the gym. Working out was such a stress reliever. She said she missed my being there, and I really appreciated the sentiments. I guess she could feel what I was facing as a caregiver, and her messages were always on time. I sounded like the women on *The Golden Girls*, thanking her for being a friend. I let her know that I appreciated all of the prayers, the talks, the laughs, and the feeling of having a sister.

Jesus be a fence! August 5, Mama was taken by ambulance to the hospital for the third time in less than three months—she had gone every month since June. Nurse Sackie had suggested calling the medic since Mama was refusing to drink water, eat food, and take her medications. When the medic got her outside, she waved to the neighbors like she was in a damn parade! Like, Mama! Girl! Stop.

Each time Mama went to the hospital, that impacted the pay for my father. See, he was being paid for being her caregiver, and I let him know that his check was going to be short again because Mama had to go back to the hospital. Technically, yes, I should have been the person receiving pay, but for some reason, guilt would set in at the very thought of being compensated for caring for my mother.

This time, she was taken to the ICU so that they could monitor her heart more closely. Selina Sprinkle, one of the ladies I'd befriended when we both worked for Walmart corporate, came to the hospital to visit. I told Selina that when I'd first met her, I thought she was from India… because her features resembled those of people from India. We laughed about that… Selina had a way of making me laugh even when I didn't want to smile.

Tavares, Quinetta, Joanne, Joanne's father, and Tavares and Joanne's twins all came to visit Mama. Joanne asked if I had eaten anything, which was the same thing Selina had asked, but I didn't have an appetite. I only wanted ginger ale and plain Fritos.

On August 7, I met with Kassandra, a representative from a hospice care service called VIA Health Partners. I felt like I was about to puke.

Life was definitely lifeing.

Kassandra explained to me that someone would be out to our home the next day to set up the hospital bed, and told me to make sure there was plenty of room for them to be able to set up. Even though my brother had said he wasn't going to help, he did help move our parents' king-size bed to the spare bedroom.

August 8 was my birthday. What a way to be spending the day.

"Hospice" was a word that scared me. I didn't know anyone who'd had longevity while in the care of hospice. So, my stomach was feeling like I had bricks in it.

The setup was smooth. The installer talked a lot, but he was quick and kind. I even tipped him. He said to me, "Usually it's our own people that don't tip. My tips usually come from areas like Davidson, Ballantyne, and other upscale areas."

I didn't care what he was saying at that point. I had tipped him enough to purchase lunch and dinner, and as far as I was concerned, he could kick rocks.

I was wishing Fatty McButter Pants were still alive. That's what I called my sister, because she worked at McDonald's and had gotten a little chubby. I missed my sister then, and still do.

I am going to set the record straight before going any further.

So, pardon me while I be clear about this particular chapter; I began writing it with the same energy Jesus had when walked into the temple in Jerusalem and flipped tables. He didn't flip tables because He lost control—He flipped them because He *had* control. He saw what was wrong. He named it. He confronted it, and He restored order.

That's exactly what I am doing in this chapter:

- Calling out what was out of alignment
- Refusing to let people twist spiritual language into harm
- Reclaiming my narrative
- Setting the record straight with authority

I am not writing in anger; I am writing in *truth*. And sometimes truth walks in, rolls up its sleeves, and says, *Yeah… this table gotta go!*

On August 9, someone named Kendra from the hospital called.

My heart was racing. I didn't know if I was breathing or passing out!

Sweat was pouring from my head, even though the air conditioner was on a comfy 73 degrees and my ceiling fan was on a high speed.

Kendra continued, "I am calling because…"

My knees buckled. I sat down. Put the phone on speaker and sat it down on the bed beside me.

I was in a daze.

"Your father is here with me," she said, "but he doesn't know where he is right now. He said that you were coming to pick him up from the hospital." He had driven himself to the hospital in his Equinox.

I asked her if I could speak with him.

"Daddy, where are you?" I said.

"I was in Concord, but now I'm at Betty's house," he answered.

"Betty?"

"Yeah, Betty. You know, Mrs. Jackson?" he said.

Listen! Mrs. Jackson had passed away in November 2021. I asked him to put Kendra back on the phone, and explained to her that Mrs. Jackson used to be the home-health aide who had taken care of my mom for decades, and that she'd passed away. I asked Kendra to keep him with her until I got someone to go pick him up from the hospital. I couldn't leave home, because I had to be here when the ambulance arrived with my mother.

I called Tavares first, but he had a doctor's appointment and was not able to help out. So I called my father's sister, Auntie Dot. I tried to hold back the tears, but I lost it. I cried so hard. Without any further questions, she went to the hospital and got her baby brother.

By the time everyone arrived, I had fixed a pan of biscuits, scrambled some eggs, and fixed some bacon and a few slices of liver mush. When my father got in the door, he reached out to give me a hug. Lord.

Have. Mercy! I felt like he knew he was safe and was back in a familiar place.

Quinetta came and would not go home. She wanted to make sure Mama was okay.

On August 12, I received a call from Joy Alfred, the social worker from VIA Health Partners. She had called to let me know that she and an RN would be out to complete their initial assessment, and to introduce themselves. They were part of the team who'd been assigned to my mother.

On August 13, we met the hospice certified nursing assistant named Angelina Tate. I'd known how to take care of my mom when she was still able to move around, not bedbound. Angelina taught me how to bathe my mother in the bed. I asked so many questions. She freely shared the knowledge she held, and she didn't make me feel stupid for not knowing basic things. (Well, basic to them, because they do these things daily; it's their bread and butter.)

Mama was usually antisocial and didn't want to talk to anyone, but she actively engaged with Angelina. I asked Angelina if she'd be the person visiting with my mom regularly, and she let me know that she was filling in for someone else. I explained to her how hard it was for my mom to open up to people, and how I could tell that she felt safe and comfortable with her.

I decided I'd call the main number for VIA Health and ask for Angelina's supervisor. They may have thought it was a distress call, but here I was on the phone trying to sound professional while crying my heart out. I let the supervisor know that we would prefer Angelina to be the CNA for my mother, based on the rapport Angelina had established with her. I apologized for crying and being so emotional.

"Never apologize for being human," the person on the phone said. "I will submit your request, and she will be the nursing assistant that does the weekly visits."

August 15, we got another visit, this time from my cousin, whose real name is Jennifer—but if you knew her, then you'd call her Vern.

I called her Jenni-Vern. Vern had driven at least 44 miles one way. When Vern learned that I needed help taking care of my mama, she showed up and led. Vern had been in the nursing field for decades before she retired, and now, she was sharing her knowledge with me. I didn't know how to do wound care, and Vern took over. She taught me how to care for the pressure wound my mother had when she was released from the hospital. Vern was faithful, she kept driving those 44 miles each way until Mama's wound had healed 100 percent.

I made the mistake of offering to pay Vern for helping me with my mom, and she told me, "Ford, I love you, cuz. But if you don't getcho black ass out my durn face talking about paying me... Hell, that's my auntie."

I was moved to tears, because someone cared enough about my mother to drive that long distance one way and not ask for anything in return. I didn't care what she said, I was going to give her some money! We sat in her car and had a chiefing session. I definitely needed ganja at that moment! I felt myself relaxing and some of the tension releasing. She stepped out of her car to smoke her Newport. While her back was turned, I put some money in her ashtray and didn't say a word. That night when she left, I told her to make sure she called or texted me to let me know she'd made it to her destination safely.

When she called, I told her, "Look in your ashtray. And don't say a word!"

"Good God all tater!" she said.

That let me know she'd found the love offering I'd given to her.

August 17, a lot of people visited with my mom. Even my brother was there. We got into an argument because I'd asked him *again* if he was going to come help out. I knew I'd need help with my father, but again he said no, and went out the back door. The argument between us escalated rapidly.

"I hate you!" my brother said, looking me square in the eyes. "I hate that you're my sister! You're so fucking stupid. Your thinking is beyond fucked up."

Then his wife chimed in and tried to tell me how I should feel. *First of motherfucking all, you married into the family! You're not in a position to tell my grown ass how I should feel about a damn thing!* All my brother had ever told people about me was that I was mean. I didn't wake up one morning and decide to be mean to people; it was a learned behavior from my parents and siblings being mean to me. So, the version of me that he had created in the minds of others was not my responsibility. I did not have to live by his definition. I was not mean. I just refused to allow people to walk all over me.

My brother tended to want to control people. Why is it that people who are not in control of their own lives try to control others? I've learned from studying psychology that people who feel out of control in their own lives often try to control others because a) control becomes a coping mechanism—when someone's own life feels chaotic, unpredictable, or unstable, they reach for the nearest thing they think they can manage, and unfortunately, that's usually another person, b) it distracts them from their own mess, c) it gives them a false sense of power—people who feel powerless internally often try to create power externally, d) they fear losing relationships they can't maintain, e) they don't trust themselves, so they don't trust anyone else, and f) it's easier to manage someone else's life than fix their own. Self-work is hard, self-awareness is uncomfortable, self-accountability is painful, but controlling someone else? That's much easier. People who are grounded, healed, and in control of themselves lead, influence, and inspire, and they do not manipulate or micromanage.

In a completely different visit when my brother's temper flared again, I decided to respond to the insults my brother had tried to throw at me. "It's funny you'd call me stupid," I told him. "Especially since I graduated college with a bachelor's degree and a master's degree; meanwhile, you're still reading on a sixth-grade level! The fuck?"

What flared his temper? He was literally upset because I didn't speak to his wife. Who the hell was he to tell me that all I had to do was speak? Before I knew it, I said, "Which one of your children can you control?

Because I'm not your damn chap. I'm 52-plus, a damn woman! Ain't shit you can tell me to do and expect me to do it! GTFOH with that!"

"Why are you cursing?" he asked me.

"Because kiss my ass, that's why!"

After that, I blocked his and his wife's phone numbers. We didn't need to talk about anything. Kick rocks! *How can you stand in my face and tell me you hate me, then want to keep talking like you ain't said shit? Where's the apology for your wrongs?*

We already didn't have a real bond, so it didn't matter that I stopped talking to him. He called twice and left angry voicemail messages, and I ignored them. Misery loves company, and I was too busy being healed to be his company! I was done with toxic people in my life.

The day he told me he hated me, I told the Lord in my prayers before I went to bed: "God, if I should die tonight, at least I'll die knowing exactly how my brother feels about me, and I forgive him. And if he should die tonight, at least he said how he felt and got that off of him, and I still forgive him. I don't have to have a relationship with him, though."

September 22, my cousin Sabrina Shine Grady (whom we called Brina) came over and plaited my mama's hair for me. I didn't have the physical capacity to do it—my mother was tender-headed, and I didn't want her to experience discomfort. Besides, Brina was a trained hairstylist and didn't mind providing extra gentle care for my mom. When I asked her how much I owed her, she told me such a low amount that I retorted, "I have to give you more than that."

"This is my auntie," Brina said. "And you cain't tell me I have to charge her more."

I nodded. Then I went and got her more than she'd asked for, and told her the rest was a tip.

Brina would come through and be with my mom on the days that I had an appointment, if she was available. I was so thankful for her being here whenever my cousin Raven Ford, who also had stepped up to help care for Mama, couldn't come.

November 9, I texted Netta:

Good morning again Quinetta. I just wanted to make sure you got the voicemail message left by Mama and me. Today is the 5th time in two months that you've been a no-call no-show. I've asked you to give us common courtesy before, just like you would if you were actually clocking in on someone's job. The only day you came this week was Tuesday & I know my ex-brother was paying you, but did you let him know you've only been here one day this week? You really made mama upset today & it was her decision to fire you. You no longer have to come over to assist because helping out over here was clearly interrupting your life. Have a good day. Love you. Mean it.

I had already figured out how to do everything by myself. I mean, after all, my father had told me when I was 15 years old that my mama was my responsibility.

On December 28, the young lady who'd been doing my locs became a person that could never touch my crown again. Up until then, she had always provided excellent services. This time, I'd made an appointment with her to get my locs cut off and my hair dyed yellow. Somehow, she misunderstood and thought the barber was cutting my locs. When she realized she was supposed to be cutting my hair, it was like she went into full tantrum mode. She started slamming shit around, and she was very rough cutting my hair; she even pulled my hair a few times when she was applying the bleach. I got chemical burns too, but I didn't complain or anything—because karma.

Being that she was a Christian, I knew that she knew better than to act that way. I also knew that vengeance was the Lord's and He would repay. I had always tipped her very well anytime I went for my appointments, so for her to behave in that manner was wild. I remained calm, kind, and cool. I thanked her for her services and left. Normally, I would make a follow-up appointment with her before my departure, but not that time. What she did was unnecessary… I still went to my barber, David (he's on IG as: trimzbytrevino).

My next color was going to be hot pink, but I went to Oasis Salon & Wellness Center to get my color done by Cheryl Thrasher-Horne. And it turned out beautiful! I returned to Cheryl to get any vanity colors done.

I was asleep when the New Year rolled around again.

January 21, 2025, I called a home care agency to learn about their respite services, because I would be going on vacation to Las Vegas in April, and I needed to know who the certified nursing assistant would be overnight. The first person they sent out wasn't the person who was supposed to come, and when she arrived, she reeked of alcohol. When she came inside, she asked me if she could take her shoes off. Before I could say a word, her damn shoes were off her feet and she was sitting on the loveseat calling her boss saying, "Hey, I'm at the client's home, and this lady is saying I'm not supposed to be here."

I took her phone and explained to the person on the other end that I had been told that someone with a different name would be here. They apologized to me, and I gave the woman back her phone. When we got to my mother's bedside, I told her that my mother was paralyzed on the left side of her body, so she would need to turn her on her left side. This bitch turned my mom on her *right* side, took her left arm and placed it on the rail, and told her to hold the rail.

"You're hurting my leg," my mom said.

"I know, you're okay," the aide responded. "Just hold on."

"This is enough of the meet and greet," I said. "I will be in touch with your office. If you want to leave now, you can."

After she was out of our home, it felt like demon spirits were floating around! I called the agency and told them that their worker smelled like she was inebriated and to never send her to our home again. Finding a good respite company was proving to be challenging. The owner assured me that the problem would be rectified. The next visit, they sent someone named Julia. Later on, the day of January 21st, I needed to find a new lash technician, and I did. Her name was Nina, and I saw her techniques along with satisfied clients on IG @lashes_by_nina_.

On January 29, my mother's case manager called, asking me if I knew that my father had been taken to the hospital at Atrium University.

"What?" I exclaimed.

I called Quinetta and asked her to stay with Mama while I drove around Charlotte trying to locate my father's car. Apparently, he had been going to the store to get some items but ended up at an auto place. The nurse from the emergency room told me where the medic had picked him up.

Can you see why I needed help? Too much for one person, but my brother had already let it be known that he wasn't going to help. He also wanted to know if my parents had life insurance, and made it seem like he was inquiring because he wanted to make sure our mom was taken care of at her funeral. When I let him know that I'd saved money from my severance package to cover her funeral services, that would've been a great time for him to offer assistance. But I think he just wanted to see if he was a beneficiary.

I called Auntie Dot again and let her know what was going on. She told me to call Jeffrey, her oldest son—Vern's twin. He let me know he had a few things he needed to take care of, and he'd go to the house immediately afterward. He also had to go to the hospital to get the Chevy Equinox key from my father so that he could drive it back to the house.

When Jeffrey got to me, he told me, "They're going to release Uncle Clyde, so Imma take his car and go get him from the hospital." I tried my best not to cry.

"I love you, cuz," he told me, giving me a hug. "It's gone be alright."

He brought my father home, but things were tense because he was wasting food again; he wouldn't eat what was on his plate. There were people who were literally starving, and he was wasting food, and it was wild. But only God truly knows what dementia had him seeing on his plate.

He had said to me one time, "I believe the seasoning you're using or the food you're cooking is what's causing me to act like that." I quit cooking, because I was not going to let him blame me for a dementia diagnosis God had already assigned to him before he was placed in his mother's womb!

Anyway, he was wound up about something when he returned home from the hospital, and told me I needed to leave. I was finishing up changing my mom's brief, and I stood 10 toes down on what I said to him: "No! You're the one that needs to leave! Running around here lying on people and saying they're spraying you with shit.

"Those are the type of lies that gets people locked up," I continued. "But let me help you understand something: Nothing in this world is worth me losing my freedom. And I most certainly will not be in lock-up because of you."

"Oh. I didn't know that!" he said, still combative.

"Well, consider yourself informed. I love my freedom, and you are not worthy of my losing mine."

Then he told me he wanted to wash clothes. It was late at night by then.

"I am not washing clothes at this hour," I said. "You can wash them in the morning."

"Why not?" he yelled.

I gave him an "if looks could kill" stare and told him, "I'm not a child any longer. I am not about to keep being disrespected by you."

He turned away from their bedroom door and went to sit in the living room.

Being a caregiver is not for the weak.

January 30, I got a call from our neighbor, Maxine saying, "Hey, is that your dad walking up the street?"

I hadn't even known he had left! My father's friend Marcheek, aka "JJ," ended up picking him from a nearby bus stop.

The next day, Maxine didn't answer when I called, and I figured maybe she was busy. So, I texted her to say:

Yesterday, when you saw him walking, he had made it down to the Shell gas station. Just so happens, JJ called his phone & I answered and asked him if he was on this side of town, would he mind looking on The Plaza to see if he'd see him. JJ saw him and picked him up from THE damn BUS STOP! He was literally getting ready to try to take the bus somewhere. He had been acting like a complete asshole since six o'clock yesterday morning! He was in here being confrontational and telling me I needed to go. first of all, out of the four children he and my mom raised, I am the ONLY ONE who takes care of both of them! Now, because I know he's scared shitless of the police, when I said I was going to call 911, he got the hell outta here! I'm capable of defending myself, if need be, but I'd rather not lay hands on him. So, when he came back home last night, he wanted to hug me like nothing had happened. He stirred up some shit & when threatened with 911, he hauled ass. Now he's acting like he got good sense! He's pissed off because he can't drive anymore. I took his keys, but he thinks my cousin has the keys.

"Okay," Maxine replied.

I think I gave her too much information at one time.

February 14 was my parents' 54th wedding anniversary, but neither one of them knew the significance of the day.

Around one o'clock in the morning, I heard a loud knock at my bedroom door, followed by, "I need some help!"

I didn't know what was waiting for me on the other side of my bedroom door.

When I got to their bedroom, the lower half of my mother's body was slightly off of her hospice bed. His dementia had him in a full episode; he had removed the bed railing from both sides of her bed. *This was too new for me... I had not been given a manual for how to care for aging parents with dementia.*

"What happened?" I asked my father. "What did you do?"

"She told me she was tired of being in that bed and wanted to get up," he said. He was definitely hallucinating, because my mother was asleep, and slept through all of that.

I called 911. I didn't touch her body.

I let the operator know that they were coming to the home of someone who showed signs of dementia or Alzheimer's, and to not come with weapons drawn. The police arrived first. I tried to tell them as calmly as I could what I knew. Which was nothing actually. The paramedics arrived, and they transported my father to Atrium University.

At 8:35 a.m. I texted JJ:

Happy Valentine's Day! Good morning, JJ. I wanted to give you an update on my dad: At one o'clock this morning, I heard a loud knock at my bedroom door, it was my dad saying he needed help. Immediately, I knew it was something with my mom! I went to their bedroom and saw that he had removed the rails from both sides of her bed. He was trying to LIFT her out of bed ad was unable to complete his task. I was going to let it go, but then I thought to myself, what if he does this again? So, as a precaution, I called 911 just as APS had asked me to do. They sent the police, fire, and medic. I tried telling them everything without crying, but I broke down. I cried but still tried to maintain my composure. The female officer asked me if I had a smartphone and allowed me to scan a QR code for different types of assistance, and she asked me if I had anyone helping me, and I told her no. Reassured her that I am not an only child; my biological brother just refuses to help! The firemen helped me to get my mom back in bed, and the paramedics took my dad to the hospital. The doctor called me and told me that there's definite signs of dementia and they'll keep him in the hospital for a couple of days to try some treatment for him. Ultimately, though, he will need to go to an assisted living facility. Today is my parent's 54th wedding anniversary, and neither of them knows it.

"Hey ok call me when you u can," JJ replied.

Ironically, that afternoon, a man named Truman stopped by. My father and my sister had done work for him in the past, but it turned out that he was not the most ethically sound person. He'd write checks to pay my sister, and when I saw the name of the payer one of her checks, I asked her, "Do you know who Harry Truman is?" I started laughing, because they certainly were not working for President Truman.

My sister retorted, "You hater! This check is legit."

I told her to take her legit check to the bank to see if they'd cash it, but before she got out of my SUV, I told her, "Google Harry Truman and see who he is."

She did that, and then looked at me and screamed, "Girl, bye! Get me out this damn bank parking lot! I am not going to jail for this shit!"

"I kept telling you and Daddy that something about that dude was not right," I told her. It's all starting to come out now. Before long, the whole truth is coming out."

My father had been trying to make fast money with Truman. I ended up having to freeze his social security number so that Truman couldn't continue trying to establish a business with him. That man had already gone to prison for conspiracy to commit health care fraud and billed Medicaid for nearly nine million dollars over a two-year time span.

I tried to protect my father, but he didn't want to listen.

I understood this to be the other type of caregiving that people don't talk too much about. But the real weight—the invisible weight— is protecting loved ones from their own decisions, shielding them from predators, managing their finances, and being the adult in the room when they still think they're in charge.

So now here was Truman in my house, lying again to my face! When I told him that my father knew he'd been using his social security number, he became very defensive. He swore he wasn't doing any of what my father had said. He also said he'd be back to check on my father once he was released from the hospital.

What do you think happened?

196

Regardless of our history, I am my father's keeper!

My brother stopped by, and that's the only reason he found out my father had gone to the hospital. We talked, but he still didn't take ownership of what he'd said, even though I had held myself accountable for my part. He never apologized. I didn't owe him an apology. I wasn't calling his phone leaving angry voicemail messages.

I was so angry with the Lord. I asked Him why I had to be the one taking care of the people who had abused me mentally, verbally, and physically when I was too young to defend myself. I asked the Lord to keep me grounded so that I would always be honorable to my parents, regardless of what they did or didn't do. I told the Lord, *not only am I their daughter; now, I am their protector.*

It's amazing how life works.

Lord knows, I was so angry with God for putting me in this position, and at the same time, I wasn't about to allow my parents to be placed in a facility.

I'd long since learned how to care for my mom without assistance from my father, Quinetta, or Jenni-Vern.

On the night of Valentine's Day, as I was changing my mother's soiled briefs, my memory reflected back to how she would beat me for wetting my bed when I was a young girl. As I mentioned earlier, I had learned from studying psychology that some children experience what is called secondary enuresis. This happens when a child starts wetting the bed *after* being dry for at least six months. Triggers can be severe stress, emotional trauma, exposure to violence, or abuse, including sexual abuse.

I had been molested. In fact, my sister had been molested, too.

I remembered the time my mother had sat Tonya and me down, when we were younger, to talk about sex. She asked us if we knew what it meant.

"Yes," I replied, "because the offender would get on top of me with my pants down, and he did the same thing to Tonya."

Tonya profusely declared it hadn't happened, though, and my mother believed her over me. Perhaps that moment had something to do with why I felt I had to prove myself when people didn't believe something I'd said.

The fact that my mother took someone else's word over mine made me feel like she didn't fully love me. Like, she loved me to a certain extent. Decades later, when I talked to my mom about that conversation, she apologized to me for not taking my word. In that moment, I understood that back then, my mom didn't know what to do with the truth I had laid out before her. I forgave my mother. I felt healed from the wound of my mother's doubt. My father, on the other hand, was not going to apologize for anything he'd done. When I reminded him that he had people thinking he was like the father on *The Cosby Show* when in reality, he was worse than Joe Jackson, father of Michael etc., he became angry. Oh well. *If you had been a better person to your family, you wouldn't receive negative feedback.*

Meanwhile, to this very day, the molester will say, "I'm the first real R. Kelly out here." As if that were something to be proud of. Ignorance is not bliss! He exhibited moral bankruptcy dressed up as bravado. Being that he has never faced his own wrongdoing, he will often try to turn it into a joke, a flex, or a twisted badge of honor. It's a way to avoid accountability. A way to pretend his harm was normal, acceptable, or even admirable.

On February 15, JJ took it upon himself to go to the hospital to check on my father. He texted me, "Hey gm I went by the hospital this am and check on him they waiting to put in in a room."

"Gm. Thank you so much," I responded. "He's still not answering his phone. I truly appreciate you!"

JJ: "Yw any time I think his phone is turned off u might hv to call over there and ask the nurse can she turn it on for I tried to turn it on I couldn't get it to come on."

Me:

His battery probably died. I called him a lot yesterday, but he never answered.

When I was able to get the nurse to give him the phone so that I could speak with him yesterday, he didn't know who I was. I pray this medicine will prevent his memory from getting worse and that he's able to return home soon. Everyone in my family that I've spoken with, has the flu so I'm not about to ask them to be here with my mom while I go see about him. You don't know how much your visit to check on him means to me. I'm so grateful.

JJ: "Yes it's in God's hands, anything u need me to do I will."

On February 18, my father was released from the hospital. The whole time, my father had thought he was in Florida supervising a new building project. He told me he had been waiting on the people to get on the bus so they could get the work finished up.

Monika, also known as Mo, was an employee at the Food Lion where my father would go to do his shopping. She would ask him what he needed, then gather up his grocery items for him while he sat on the bench waiting for her to return. She took care of him when he was at that store. On February 26, she texted me, "How is Mr. Clyde, we haven't seen him in the store lately? I told the crew I would text you and check in."

I replied:

Hello, Mo. Hru today? Just a heads up, if you're at work today: My pop's will be there later today to exchange the gallon of milk he purchased. He said he had the receipt, but I never saw it. He said he couldn't remember the name of the milk that he usually gets (Lactaid), so he bought some 2% milk instead. Later on today, his godson, JJ will bring him to the store to do the exchange, & my pop asked me if I'd let you know he was coming so that you could help him. I know he needs to get the money order for rent, so would you mind assisting him with that also? I cannot leave them in the house alone. He has dementia and so does my mom, and she's bedridden on home-hospice. Thank you in advance.

Without hesitation, Mo responded, "No problem sis! I will take care of him. He don't need a receipt. I leave at 3." Look at how God works, because not only did she make sure he got his milk, but she came and picked him up from the house! JJ caught up with them at the store and brought my father back home. Mo showed me that she's a person with a good heart, and I am forever grateful for her stepping in when I couldn't.

It takes a village.

It is beyond terrifying to watch a loved one have dementia, see them mentally and physically react to their hallucinations. I'd always believed the full moon was beautiful enough to gaze at in admiration, but I don't know if I feel that way any longer, because the full moon has an impact on persons with dementia. I learned this valuable lesson from observing both of my parents.

As I write this, my parents are both still alive, and I'm still trying to get a reputable respite company here so that I can take an overdue vacation. I am literally exhausted. And not just because of the physical work, or the countless hours of emotional work, but because 24 hours a day, I am constantly vigilant. I am the cook. I am the laundromat attendant. I am the pharmacist. I am the adult brief changer (for my mother). I am the nurturer; every time I change my mother's briefs, I kiss her forehead, because I don't know if it's the last time I'll get to say "I love you." She probably gets sick of hearing me say that I love her and kissing her forehead, but does she even know what I'm doing? I am the nail tech providing spa services. I am the beautician washing my bedbound mother's hair. I am the nurse, documenting symptoms and providing ointments. I am the supporter. I am the protector. I am my mother's keeper. I am my father's keeper. I am unpaid. My compensation is knowing that I'm doing the best I can each day for my parents.

April 8, 2025, I went to Las Vegas, because I needed a break! It was Joanne and Tavares's first time going. Netta and I had gone for my 50th birthday, and she was joining again this time. Raven stayed with my parents every day while I was away, and Julia from the respite company stayed with them overnight. How one person was able to work for 16 hours straight is between that person and Medicaid! My cousin Raven was the real MVP for showing up when I was in a pinch. She even learned how to make the shakes for my mom the same way I did. My mother did not like swallowing her pills, so I would add them to her Ensure Plus drinks. I would doctor up the Ensure, though. I would blend in a Little Debbie Strawberry Shortcake Roll to enhance the flavor and make it more appealing for my mom. But mostly, it was to mask the taste of medication.

Medicaid and Medicare don't pay for things like Ensure Plus, which makes the cost of being a caregiver expensive. But because that drink is all my mother will consume, I would sell my right leg to keep her nourished. Even though my mom's appetite is minimal, she still gets constipated each month. But instead of giving her the laxatives that have been prescribed for her, I give her two Activia probiotic drinkable yogurts in strawberry or vanilla as needed. They give my mom relief.

While we were in Vegas, we went to a dispensary called Cookies on Flamingo Road. I got a vape pen, Netta got gummies, and Tavares got flowers. I decided I was going to be grown up and try a gummy. Netta gave me one, and I ate the whole thing. Twelve minutes later, I was lit! We were at a timeshare presentation, and all of a sudden, the dude in front of me started looking like the Geico caveman. I burst into laughter and couldn't stop. Everyone around me was laughing without knowing why.

"What's wrong with her?" the guy asked Netta.

"This Smurf gave me a gummy!" I answered, snorting while laughing.

"How much did you eat?" Netta asked me, leaning over.

"I got a big back. I ate the whole thing!"

"Oh shit!" Netta said, sounding panicked. "You were only supposed to eat half."

"What a fine time to tell me," I said.

I was so high. Oh my gosh! I swear on my bottom dollar, I will never, not ever, in this lifetime eat another gummy! That thing was smaller than a Starburst, and I was high until later that evening, when we went to a comedy show.

May 20, I completed my online application for Claremont Lincoln University, which offers a master's in human resources management. I love working in HR, and I figured it was time to add some fancy book learning to my on-the-job experiences. I chose this college because it's in direct alignment with the SHRM certification.

The next day, I received an email: "Congratulations! Angela, you have been accepted into the program."

I decided to give up ganja so that I could be fully focused on my upcoming studies. Look at me! Once upon a time, my grade-point average was *less than one*! Now, I'd been accepted into CLU. July 7 was the first day of class. My personal goal at this school was clear: maintain a 3.8 GPA or higher.

***

August 4, I had a dream where Quinetta and I were at someone's house getting ready to enjoy ladies' night at a club. Everyone except Netta and me had a drink in their hand, ready to turn up at the club. I kept looking for my other shoe, and then I was going to go get in the shower. Just as I found my shoe and headed to the bathroom, Netta yelled from inside, "I'm about to take my shower." I decided to go outside and get some fresh air, and I was just looking at how beautiful nature was. Then Netta came out of the house, walked up to me, and said, "I just got a call that Mama died."

In my dream, I could feel myself changing positions in my bed, as if I were trying to fight something off of me. I looked down at Netta and said, "Say what? Excuse me." She said, "Nah. It was me." She threw up two fingers, the peace sign, turned, and walked away.

I felt like I had been shocked with something, because I was jolted awake.

I sat on the side of my bed for the longest time, trying to shake that dream. It was a little past four o'clock in the morning. I should've been asleep, but I couldn't force myself to close my eyes.

It felt like something heavy had come upon me. My palms were sweating. I wanted to text Netta right then, but it was too early, so I waited until eight o'clock. Every day, Netta and I would send each other a text message to say "good morning" and "I love you."

This time, I didn't get a response, and I low-key began panicking.

It felt like a lump was in my throat. I couldn't tell if it was nerves or a hot flash, which I'd begun to get regularly.

At 10:39 a.m., the incoming call displayed Joanne's name. I answered before the second ring, and Joanne asked, "Have you talked to Quinetta? I keep calling that li'l heffa, but her ass not answering the phone. Actually, my calls are going straight to voicemail."

I cleared my throat and tried to say as strongly as I could, "Based on the dream I had, go find her."

"Oh shit! Angie! You're scaring me," she exclaimed.

"Go find her," I repeated. "I am going to make a phone call, and I'll get right back in touch with you."

I called Ree-Ree, Netta's bestie, and told her about the dream I had and that Netta was not answering the phone.

"What?" Ree-Ree said. "Let me make a phone call, and I'll call you right back."

When she called back 15 minutes later, my heart was racing.

I heard Ree let out a screeching type of cry: "Angie! They said she's *deeeeeaaad*. Quinetta is dead."

It felt like the wind had been knocked out of me.

I called Joanne and gave her the news.

When Joy Alfred (I called her Minister Joy), the hospice social worker arrived, I told her about the dream I'd had.

"You are a seer," she told me.

"A who-er?" I said.

She explained to me the Biblical reference and told me that it was a powerful gift.

"Who gifted me?" I asked, in total seriousness. "I didn't ask for this."

"Ma'am! You have something that people pray their whole lives for," Minister Joy said. "God chose you to have this gift."

I admitted to her that it scared me to see things in dreams come to pass. She shared some Scriptures with me, but my mind was in a fog. Was this another prophecy? Or was she just speaking spiritually about what she saw in me?

Quinetta was stubborn and hadn't wanted to take her blood pressure medication. She'd had a heart attack and passed instantly.

I received a phone call via the Messenger app from the girl who enjoyed drama—the one who'd grown up with us in Earle Village.

I ignored the call, because I did not want to talk to a fake friend. I'd arrived at a stage in my life where I realized she could be my friend in the *flesh* but my enemy in spirit. Enemies do not always come with opposition; sometimes they come with proximity. Same circle. Same access. Different spirits. That's why God will create distance without drama. No argument. No exposure. Just separation. God was not punishing me; He was and is preserving me. Not everyone close to me is assigned to go with me. Some people are tolerated in one season but restricted in the next. When God removed that girl quietly, it was not rejection; it was protection.

The girl who enjoyed drama was a very selfish person—even after I'd given her a lot! She was dismissive. Judgmental. Illustrated a performative spirituality. Had zero compassion, zero awareness of what I was actually carrying. Life had taught me that after a certain age, people should realize that they are no longer a product of their environment; it becomes a personal choice to continue living in the toxic, drama-filled way that they do.

Today, I choose to be stress-free.

I also choose to be free of fake friendships.

I have spent too much of my life trying to fit in, when in reality, I was built Ford-tough, to stand out! Truth is, I can't fit in and stand out simultaneously, so I have decided to be outstanding!

August 13, my phone lit up showing a call coming in from Julia, the aide from the respite care agency.

"Hey, Miss Angie," she said, "I am not available on the 19th. Being there with your mom is a waste of my time. I can be at other clients' homes making money, but I'm sitting there with her all day, losing money. What I can do is bring my niece with me to sit with your mom while I go get the extra hours. I will still bathe her and give her her medicine, but my niece will sit with her until I return."

I abruptly told her no.

"Are you sure?" she replied. "I mean, I was going to take my niece by the office today to fill out an application. She knows how to do the work."

I said no again and hung up the phone. The fact that she'd been comfortable enough to suggest her niece sitting in for her told me she'd already done that.

I called the agency and told them what had happened and asked them to cancel all outstanding service requests. When I told the office manager about what Julia had said, she responded, "Even if her niece came to fill out an application and was hired today, she still wouldn't have been able to sit with your mom. The aide who is assigned to be with your mother that day is the one that has to be there the entire time."

Whatever the case, I let them know that I'd learned that I could not do business with all Black-owned companies. I called my mother's caseworker to inform her of what'd happened, and she put me in contact with Right Touch NC. I spoke with the owner, Tori, and she came out the same day to do a meet and greet.

August 15, my belated birthday present to myself was to address the awkward feeling I had of dining alone. Thanks to watching the founder and lead instructor of iTeachiTutor, Walidah Staley as she travels the world fearlessly. Her solo travels inspired me to step out and treat myself to a meal at LongHorn Steakhouse. I will solo travel eventually someday. Quinetta and I were supposed eat at LongHorn for my birthday; sadly, she didn't get to join me.

I also gifted myself with overcoming my fear of getting ombré service for my brows. Up until the 15th, I stuck with henna because Ashley at InherGlow Brows & Beauty always did a phenomenal job. Every time I went, I'd ask her questions about ombré, and she was always so kind and professional — never making me feel uneducated for not knowing the process. When I finally decided to book the ombré service, I went to IG and searched. I watched before-and-after videos of Ashley's clientele, and I knew I had to book with her. Best eyebrows decision I've ever made. Don't believe me? Check her out: www.inherglowbeauty.com.

Quinetta's funeral was on August 30. So many people asked me if I'd let my mother know of Netta's passing, and I said, "No. She has a weak heart. Why would I tell her something to upset her?" If my mother were to ask about her, I'd simply say that I hadn't spoken with her in a while. Which, technically, wouldn't be a lie.

***

October 28, Hurricane Melissa, a powerful Category 5 hurricane, made landfall in Jamaica. I had a cruise planned for the week of Christmas. Quinetta was supposed to be on that cruise with me. I didn't mind a solo trip; I just didn't know who'd make sure my parents got their medications. How could I have enjoyed my trip if my mind was back home in Charlotte, worried about them? The social worker from hospice, the one I call Minister Joy, reminded me that I needed to take a vacation, and I needed to care for myself first. I appreciated the concern, but the reality is, I will take trips when I no longer have the responsibility of being a full-time caregiver. The chaplain from hospice,

Pastor Major A. Stewart (also a published author—find his work on Amazon), prayed a prayer so strong that it felt like weight was shifted. I had purchased some of his books and asked him to sign them for me.

"You know, I'm signing my books for you, but I believe there's a book that you'll be signing for me one day," he said, smiling.

I canceled my cruise. I was sad about it, but at the same time, I had peace in my heart and mind, because no one would have looked after my parents the same as I do. I also got a refund on my flight. I ended up canceling another trip to Daytona Beach, Florida, in March 2026 for the same reason.

What my journey has taught me is that *only God* can take someone who was wounded by their parents and still give them the heart to show up with compassion, gentleness, and honor. The exhaustion that I feel is the weight of a promise kept to them.

***

February 14, 2026, I stood by my mother's side holding her right hand when suddenly, I heard her take her last two breaths. I thank God for being able to be there with my mother as she transitioned. I was so afraid of her passing away while I was at an appointment, in the shower, or asleep. If I had to redo life as a caregiver for my mom, I would complete the task without hesitation. Alexander Funeral Home handled her memorial service, and they did a magnificent job.

## Author's Bio

Angie Ford is a memoirist, a caregiver, and a daughter who loves fiercely and advocates without apology. Her voice was shaped by the difficult and defining events that unfolded throughout her life, and she wrote this memoir as a testimony that allowed her to heal from everything that tried to break her. Angie stands for boundaries, emotional clarity, truth, and unwavering advocacy. Each day, she prays for feet that follow God, hands that serve with purpose, and a heart that loves others with the same grace she has received.